MEN-AT-ARMS SERIES

EDITOR: PHILIP WARNER

Montcalm's Army

Text by MARTIN WINDROW

Colour plates by MICHAEL ROFFE

OSPREY PUBLISHING LIMITED

Published in 1973 by
Osprey Publishing Ltd, P.O. Box 25,
707 Oxford Road, Reading, Berkshire
© Copyright 1973 Osprey Publishing Ltd

The author would like to record his gratitude to those
who gave valuable help during the preparation of
this book, notably G. A. Embleton, R. G. Windrow
and P. Gidaly. The editor of *Tradition* was kind enough
to give his permission for the reproduction of certain
material first published in past issues of that magazine. The main source works consulted were, not
surprisingly, Francis Parkman's monumental work
Montcalm and Wolfe, first published in 1884 and
currently available in a 1964 edition from Eyre &
Spottiswoode; and the series of colour plates of
French troops published by M. Eugène Leliepvre,
the much-respected French authority.

ISBN 0 85045 144 2

Printed in Great Britain by
Jarrold & Sons Ltd, Norwich

Introduction

The Peace of Aix-la-Chapelle in 1748 did not long postpone the final confrontation between Britain and France in North America. The whole continent, with the exception of the thirteen British colonies on the east coast and residual Spanish holdings in the far south and west was claimed by Louis XV as 'New France'. With strategic areas of settlement along the St Lawrence and the Great Lakes, and up the Mississippi from Louisiana on the Gulf coast, France could throw a noose around the Thirteen Colonies. Already penned behind the natural barrier of the Appalachians, their westward expansion could be frustrated by this chain of French forts, blockhouses, trading posts, and missions, and, most important in practice, by the 'buffer' of Indian tribes manipulated by France.

France's weakness lay in numbers. The noose looked impressive on a map, but was only lightly woven. In all her American possessions France had only about 80,000 colonists, some 55,000 of them in Canada. The bulk of the remainder were in Acadia (roughly, modern Nova Scotia) and far-off Louisiana; the chain of settlements up the Mississippi was very weakly populated. Ironically, the Roman Catholic Church in France was busily persecuting the Huguenots – a resourceful and able section of the population, admirably suited for pioneer ventures – while refusing them the chance to emigrate; the colonies were reserved for orthodox Catholics only.

If dogmatic bigotry denied the colonies much-needed new blood, at least it helped ensure that what colonists there were followed the path of obedience. Canada was Old France in microcosm, a feudal Catholic state transplanted to the wilderness. The Governor-General had his little Versailles at Quebec. The great hereditary *seigneurs* held huge land-grants from the Crown, and the docile peasantry worked them. All education – and the means to withhold it if convenient – lay with the Church. But while Canada had many of the vices of the mother country, including a deeply entrenched corruption which hamstrung the colonial administration, at least the local gentry had escaped the effeminacy of many of their French cousins, and the peasants the abject misery of those

Engraving of an officer saluting with his fusil. Note particularly the gorget worn by this figure, and the hearts stitched into the coat-tails. This, and the other engravings in the same series which appear in this book, are from the *Exercice de l'Infanterie Françoise* of 1757. They were drawn by an officer of the Grenadiers de la Garde named Baudouin, and officers and men wear the uniform of that unit.

at home. This was a frontier community, whether feudal or not, and a certain frontier hardiness was its saving grace.

The Thirteen Colonies had no shortage of population; by about 1750 there were 1,600,000 of them. In vivid contrast to their French counterparts, however, they were an unruly and uncoordinated brood whose domestic squabbles did them untold damage again and again. The painful birth-pangs of democracy could hardly have come at a worse time. When France began to move against them, and their London-appointed governors went to the colonial legislatures with bills for the raising of men and money for vital defence measures, the colonies resisted what they were inclined to interpret as a devious plot to endanger their civil liberties. United only in their ultimate allegiance to King George, the colonies viewed each other with indifference or downright suspicion. They were mentally and physically remote; their hysterical debates dragged on with a blissful disregard for the actual threat to their future, and any parsimonious vote of men and means was passed only when the fair-haired scalps were already dry on the lodge-poles of the Abenaki villages. For France had decided to stunt the growth of the British colonies by the easiest and most effective means available – the stirring up of the savage tribes who inhabited the forested hills

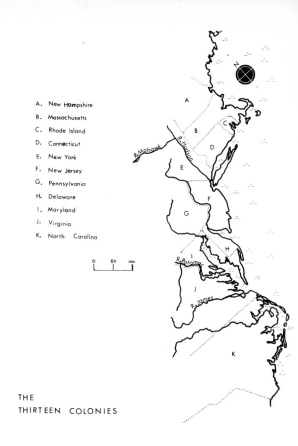

A. New Hampshire
B. Massachusetts
C. Rhode Island
D. Connecticut
E. New York
F. New Jersey
G. Pennsylvania
H. Delaware
I. Maryland
J. Virginia
K. North Carolina

THE THIRTEEN COLONIES

along the western fringe of the British settlements. With the exception of the New Englanders, and particularly the dour Yankees of Massachusetts, the colonists were in no state to defend themselves.

For her major effort France concentrated on the Ohio Valley, linchpin of the planned anti-British belt along the frontier. The Indians of the region included Delawares, Wyandots, Shawanoes, Mingoes, Nipissings, Ottawas, and Abenakis; and in recent years the incursions of British colonial fur-traders had seriously damaged French influence – and trade – in the area. The first step was for officers of the 'colony troops' (the *Compagnies Franches de la Marine*, the local French *gendarmerie*) to travel throughout the area lecturing the tribes on their duty to the Great French Father Across the Sea, and on the perfidy of the Virginian and Pennsylvanian traders. At the same time the Jesuit missionaries launched a great spiritual and political drive, based on their missions at La Présentation, Lorette, St Francis, and elsewhere. Energetic priests, such as the formidable Abbé Picquet, lured the tribes from their villages, vulnerable to the British traders, into great camps

Sketch-map of the eastern half of the North American continent in the 1750s, from the coast to the Mississippi. French possessions surround the Thirteen Colonies and prevent westwards expansion. (R.G.W.)

around the missions. These were chapels, forts, and trading stations combined, staffed by both priests and soldiers. The missionaries were as much political agents as clergymen. In their fortified settlements they preached a version of the Gospel which gave the savages a proper grasp of the utter evil of the British, without bothering their simple heads with niceties of historical accuracy or moral judgment. Here they carried on a brisk trade in furs; and here they organized war-parties of Indians and hardly less barbaric Canadian bush-rangers, to harry the British frontier settlements. Here brandy barrels were tomahawked open beside the fires on which were roasted the gifts of French cattle. Here the war-belt was passed from hand to hand, and the war-song was sung, while cynical French officers yawned behind their hands at the interminable speeches of self-praise in which the Indians delighted. Here the fine Charleville muskets and the bright new hatchets were distributed, the powder and ball, the steel scalping-knifes. And here the satiated tribesmen returned, fresh scalps reeking at their belts, herding half-crazed white women to a life of slavery, or prisoners destined for a hideous death within ear-shot of the uncaring French agents. It was a strange gospel that the Abbé Picquet preached, but it proved palatable. French influence grew, the tribes became infected with scalp-fever as never before, and the British traders were expelled. Even some clans of the Five Nations were seduced from the long-standing amity between Iroquois and British.

The First Round

The arrival in 1752 of the new Governor-General, Duquesne, opened a new phase. Until now the struggle for supremacy had been carried on at second hand, with Indians; now French uniforms would be seen on the frontier. Duquesne sent an expedition of colony troops and militia down Lake Erie in the spring of 1753, and established forts at Presqu'ile and Le Bœuf. Some 300 men garrisoned them in the winter of 1753-4, when an embassy from Virginia, led by a young Major George Washington, arrived to demand French withdrawal from lands '. . . so notoriously known to be the property of the Crown of Great Britain'. He received an evasive answer, great courtesy to his face, and a war-party on his trail as he struggled through the frozen forest on a nightmare return journey. The Indians of the Ohio Valley were positively fawning on the French. Governor Dinwiddie of Virginia, a tireless old watchdog for His Majesty's interests, obtained permission and – at length – means to combat the threat. His provincial troops tried to establish a fort near the Forks of the Ohio, but were chased off in April 1754 by 500 French, who promptly erected the

The Ohio Valley region, cockpit for battle throughout the war. George Washington and the Virginia Regiment were beaten by the French at Fort Necessity in 1754; Braddock and the 44th and 48th Foot were massacred on the Monongahela near Fort Duquesne in 1755; and Forbes eventually took over the deserted remains of Fort Duquesne in 1758. The normal route of French access was down the Allegheny from the settlements on the southern shore of Lake Erie; that of the British and provincials, up the Potomac from Alexandria. The main Indian tribes of the area are indicated here, although it was a time of great freedom of movement among the native population. (R.G.W.)

5

formidable Fort Duquesne on the site so conveniently cleared. In May a confused skirmish led French and Virginian troops into a fire-fight for the first time; and although it was to be two years before war was officially declared between France and Britain, matters now developed on the frontier as if the declaration had already been made.

In July 1754 the Virginia provincials were blooded, and humiliated, by a large force of colony troops and militia at 'Fort Necessity', an entrenched camp near Great Meadows. Throughout the Thirteen Colonies alarmed governors went to their assemblies for grants to raise men to defend the newly threatened frontier. Those worthy bodies fulfilled French hopes, by doing all they could to thwart this necessary provision. Only Massachusetts, energetic as always, answered the trumpet-call promptly. Of the others, some rejected the bills out of hand; some took refuge in a smug pacifism; some prevaricated; and some gleefully added such constitutionally controversial riders that the fuming governors could not possibly

Baudouin plate showing a soldier of the front rank of the battle line in the drill position, 'Ready your arms!'

approve the bills as a whole. Meanwhile alarm was growing in London. Officially there was peace; it suited the devious minds of Whitehall admirably for the far-off colonies to pay for their own defence. On the other hand it would never do for these unruly children to acquire skill through familiarity at raising regiments of armed men. It seemed unavoidable, even to the dim-witted Duke of Newcastle (under whose rule England currently blundered along) that regular troops should be sent to the Americas. No sooner had the news reached Versailles than Louis XV, too, prepared an expeditionary force. Both governments protested their peaceful intentions; and while the diplomats smiled and lied, the soldiers were mustered. Britain had a large and formidable navy, but a weak and ill-led army. France had a weak navy, but a large army. Its leadership was not up to the standard achieved in the days of the great Turenne and Saxe, thanks to the meddling of La Pompadour, but it was a formidable instrument.

Britain, whose interests would be served best by hasty surgical action in the Ohio Valley, got her fleet to sea first; about 1,000 men of the 44th and 48th Foot, under Major-General Edward Braddock, took ship from Cork in January 1755. By April his army lay around Alexandria, Virginia, and recruiting was under way – both to bring the regular battalions up to strength and to provide provincial support. Braddock, Dinwiddie, and Governor Shirley of Massachusetts had agreed on a strategic plan. Braddock was to march on Fort Duquesne with his redcoats, the most powerful force on the continent. (The French convoy still lay at Brest, dogged by delays.) An expedition of New England provincials was to cauterize, at long last, the running sore of French activity in Nova Scotia. New England, New York, and New Jersey provincials would march on the key French position of Crown Point on the shore of Lake Champlain, under the command of William Johnson of New York; he was a popular and influential backwoods baron with a notable skill at managing relations with the Mohawk Indians, who worshipped him. The French post at Niagara, on the southern shore of Lake Ontario, would be taken by Shirley with two new provincial regiments taken into the King's pay, and named 'Shirley's' and 'Pepperell's'. Canada would thus

George Washington, whose Virginian provincial troops fought the action which sparked off open hostilities in 1754, was present at Braddock's massacre during the abortive advance on Fort Duquesne in 1755, and finally saw the abandoned ruins of the fort captured by Forbes's column in the winter of 1758-9. This interesting old print purports to show him saluting the raising of the British flag over the fort. It is correct in including Highlanders, provincials and scouts on the scene, but incorrect in its implication that Washington was responsible for the success of the campaign. In fact the fort was taken over in the depths of a snowbound winter, and its capture may be attributed equally to the poor French supply situation after reverses on Lake Ontario: the neglect of the Indian alliance by the commandant: and the determination of the gallant Forbes himself. (P. H. Gidaly)

be cut off from her western outposts, which must perish.

On 6 July 1755 an Indian scout reported to Captain Contrecœur of the *Compagnies Franches*, commandant of Fort Duquesne, that a huge body of British was approaching. This was Braddock's column; it consisted of 1,200 redcoats with engineers and artillery, some Virginian 'bluecoats' under George Washington, and much baggage and impedimenta. It was forced to travel slowly as 300 axemen carved a track for it through the wilderness. Contrecœur had but a few companies of the *Compagnies Franches* and some militia – tough forest fighters, but no match for redcoats trained to European standards. Panic threatened, but Contrecœur remained steady. He ordered barrels of powder and ball opened and set at the gates; then he went to talk to his allies – 800 warriors of the Hurons, the Ojibways, the Abenakis and Caughnawagas, the Mingoes and Shawanoes, even some Ottawas led, it is said, by the great Pontiac himself. . . .

The story of Braddock's Massacre is well known, and has no lengthy place here. The column was divided into an advance party, under Lieutenant-Colonel Thomas Gage, and a main force, under Braddock. At about noon on the 9th the head of the column ran into the French force in thick woods some seven miles from Fort Duquesne, near the fords of the Monongahela River. The French had about 800 Indians with about thirty-six French officers scattered among them – many greased and painted like their allies – including particularly the gallant Captain de Beaujeu and the guerilla, Langlade. They were supported by seventy-two men of the *Compagnies Franches* and

7

Sketches from contemporary portraits of (left) Daniel de Beaujeu, who fell leading the Indian attack on Braddock's column in 1755, and (right) the Chevalier de Lévis, Montcalm's second-in-command and successor. (G. A. Embleton).

Braddock fell shot through the lungs as he tried to order a retreat by the survivors; he had already had four horses shot from under him, and his courage, at least, was never in question. He died later, and the army marched over his grave to hide it from the Indians. Only about twenty-three officers and 460 men escaped alive and able to walk, out of 1,450 odd. The wounded were abandoned on the field, and a white captive at Fort Duquesne recorded nightmare scenes in the Indian camps for days afterwards.

The survivors, still ashen with the memory of what they had seen, arrived at length at Fort Cumberland. They were soon pulled right back to Philadelphia, and the frontier was left naked to the French and their jubilant savages. The shock in the Thirteen Colonies was as great as had been their confidence when the apparently invincible redcoats had marched off. In New France all was rejoicing, little dimmed by the news that Acadia (Nova Scotia) had at last been cleared of their supporters with a terrible efficiency by some 2,000 Massachusetts men and a small force of British regulars. (This had occurred in June 1755; and in the months to follow Britain was to transport every peasant in Acadia who would not swear fealty to King George – rough justice, but long withheld.)

Far to the north another little drama was in preparation, which would also go down in American folklore. The new Governor of Canada, the unpleasant Marquis de Vaudreuil, had now

some 140 militiamen. They suffered badly for the first few minutes of the action, as the redcoats swung into line and charged with the bayonet. Then the Indians spread along the flanks and began to snipe and to rush in to cut off stragglers. In minutes the British were being driven back like bewildered cattle, unable to see the enemy who were firing into their ranks from behind thick cover. The advance party retreated, the main force advanced, the two collided; and for three hours confused and increasingly panic-stricken knots of redcoats blazed away at trees and banks of powder-smoke, while their officers pushed them into the useless line formation, and the provincials took cover behind trees to fight back Indian-fashion. Braddock was not a stupid man, though history has not been kind to him. He simply knew no other way of fighting. Ben Franklin said of him: 'This General was, I think, a brave man, and would probably have made a good figure in some European war, but he had too much self-confidence; too high an opinion of the validity of regular troops; too mean a one of Americans and Indians.'

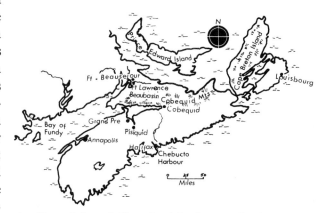

Acadia and the neighbouring islands, 1755. In that year a force of Massachusetts provincials landed at the head of the Bay of Fundy and took Fort Beausejour, the centre from which trouble had been fomented among the French peasants and the Micmac Indians for many years. (R.G.W.)

arrived and taken over from Duquesne, and with him he brought regulars to the number of about 1,600 under a German general, Baron Dieskau, who had served with Saxe. Originally the convoy had carried about 3,000 of the white-coated *troupes de terre*; some 1,000 of the battalions of Artois and Bourgogne had been landed to reinforce the Louisbourg garrison on Île Royale – now completely cut off from Canada by the purging of Acadia – and another 400 had been captured at sea. Admiral Boscawen had managed to ambush the vessels *Alcide* and *Lys* off Cape Race in June, capturing four companies each of the battalions of La Reine and La Sarre.

Papers found on the field of Braddock's Massacre warned the French of Johnson's impending attack on Crown Point, so Dieskau's force was sent down Lake Champlain in canoes and *bateaux*, with support totalling about 2,000 colony troops, Canadian militia, and Indians. Leaving the baggage at Crown Point they marched on to the promontory of Ticonderoga, commanding the narrows where Lake George and Lake Champlain joined, and where rapids forced all travellers to manhandle their boats over a portage track. From here they could cover all practical routes of advance on Crown Point.

Johnson, with an army of 2,500 provincials from several colonies, was now moving north from the settled areas of the Hudson and Mohawk Valleys. The last major settlement was the Dutch fur-trading capital of Albany, a fortified frontier city. The force reached a temporary stockade on the site later named Fort Edward late in August, and in September cut a fourteen-mile road to the southern tip of Lake George. Some 500 men remained at the stockade; some 2,000 with a fluctuating force of Indians camped on the lake near the site of the later Fort William Henry. Here they stayed while boats were brought up for the projected trip to Crown Point.

On 7 September scouts brought Johnson word of tracks to the east. Dieskau, with 216 regulars (two companies each of the battalions of Languedoc and La Reine), 680 Canadians, and 600 Indians, was moving south to attack the stockade, and not until that night did they realize that there was a camp on Lake George. They cut the road between the stockade and the camp, and moved

The Marquis de Vaudreuil, last French Governor-General of Canada, and Montcalm's bitterest enemy. (From a contemporary portrait)

north along it. Warned on the 8th of the approach of about 1,000 of Johnson's force from the camp, Dieskau set a trap. Halting the regulars on the road he sent the Indians and militia forward through the trees on each flank. Their first surprise volley crumpled the head of the provincial column like a pack of cards, and the regulars came tramping into sight to drive the shaken provincials back up the road. After initial panic they made a good withdrawal by 'fire and movement', and regained the barricades of tree-trunks, boats, and wagons which Johnson had been throwing up around the camp since hearing the gunfire on the wind. This action was ever afterwards known as 'The Bloody Morning Scout'. It was followed that afternoon by 'The Battle of Lake George'. For four hours the French regulars charged the barricades, suffering severely from Johnson's three cannon, while irregulars of both sides skirmished in the thick bush in front of the perimeter. Eventually the French were beaten off with 228 losses, including half the French regulars and nearly all the officers. Provincial losses were about 260. Dieskau, wounded repeatedly in the legs and pelvis, was captured, and narrowly escaped being roasted alive and eaten by Johnson's Mohawk allies. The stoic German, who was never fully to recover, paid his rustic victors a pretty compliment: that in the morning they had fought like good boys, at noon like men, and in the afternoon like devils. He had nothing but rolling curses for his own unreliable Indians and Canadians.

Johnson did not develop his movement towards Crown Point, and stayed where he was. The French retreated to Ticonderoga. Far to the south-west a serious threat to the integrity of the line of French holdings was removed when Governor

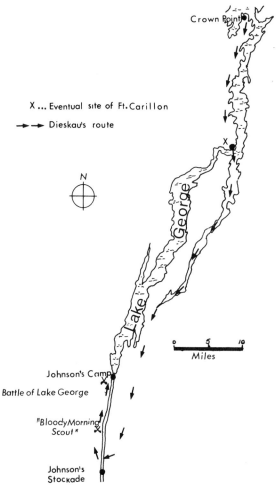

X ... Eventual site of Ft. Carillon

→→ Dieskau's route

The Lake George–Lake Champlain area; the lakes formed a water highway between Albany and the British settlements on the Mohawk and the Hudson, to the south, and the Richelieu River and Montreal, to the north. This region was therefore the most hotly contested of all during the Seven Years War. The routes and positions shown on this sketch-map refer to Dieskau's defeat at the Battle of Lake George in 1755; note that Fort William Henry later rose on the site of 'Johnson's Camp', and Fort Edward on the site of 'Johnson's Stockade'. (R.G.W.)

Shirley failed to press his expedition against Niagara. All in all the French had reason to be well pleased with the results gained for little price. Braddock's Massacre led to an autumn and early winter of sheer horror along the lonely marches of the Thirteen Colonies. Flushed with victory, the tribesmen took up the hatchet with a vengeance, and tragedy visited many a lonely little settlement in the clearings of the primeval forest. Dumas, the new commandant at Fort Duquesne, reported:

'. . . I have succeeded in ruining the three adjacent provinces, Pennsylvania, Maryland and Virginia, driving off the inhabitants, and totally destroying the settlements over a tract of country thirty leagues wide, reckoning from the line of Fort Cumberland. M. de Contrecœur had not been gone a week before I had six or seven different war-parties in the field at once, always accompanied by Frenchmen. So far we have lost only two officers and a few soldiers, while the Indian villages are full of prisoners of every age and sex. The enemy has lost far more since the battle than on the day of his defeat.'

To do them credit, it must be said that Dumas and his officers made genuine attempts to limit the barbarity of the savages against their prisoners, but there was little they could do. The frontiers continued to endure a reign of terror until the winter of 1755–6 brought large-scale campaigning to a close.

Montcalm

After such incidents of horror it is strange to record that it was only in May 1756 that war was formally declared. The delicate balance of power in Europe was trembling, and far more was at stake than the future of New France and the Thirteen Colonies. At Versailles all eyes were turned to the traditional battlegrounds of Europe; ignoring the vital potential of the American empire in terms of trade and world power, France persisted in regarding the war there as a sideshow. Nevertheless, however boring the problem might be for the men – and women – who had appointments in their gift, France must clearly have a new general in the colony. Dieskau was still struggling toward an imperfect recovery in British captivity. None of the court favourites saw much prospect of glory and advancement in such an uncomfortable command, and at length the choice fell on an obscure brigadier, six times wounded, a front-line colonel in the late wars in Bohemia and Italy. He had few important connections, no wealth, and – if one could credit such a thing – preferred to slum it on his threadbare little estates in the south, surrounded by pigs and children, rather than circulate with the gilded moths of Versailles. Obviously the man was born to do jobs like this.

Louis-Joseph, Marquis de Montcalm-Gozon de Saint-Véran, was just forty-four years old, a short man running to middle-aged chubbiness. He was a Mediterranean character, warm and open, with lively dark eyes, thick black brows, and a great predatory beak of a Roman nose. He was a shade impulsive, but always considerate to his subordinates, a humorous and energetic man who tended to talk too fast and laugh too loud when excited. He was one of those rare generals whose men love him as well as respecting him. When he fell, common soldiers who had seen him, from a distance, three or four times in their lives, would weep like children. He was a leader of men, whose officers were consumed with a fierce loyalty to him, a readiness to champion him against any detractor. His surviving letters to his family show him to be a tender husband, and a loving father; the letters and journals of his staff officers show that his affectionate nature was appreciated.

Born in the family *château* at Candiac, near Nîmes, in 1712, Louis was the son of country nobility with acres but little cash. By the time he joined the Régiment d'Hainault as an ensign in 1727, a pedantic tutor had managed to instil a love of books and a mildly academic leaning, though never a legible French hand or 'a proper docility'. In 1729 his father bought him a captaincy, and six years later died, leaving Louis the title and considerable debts. A marriage was arranged which brought him property, some connections,

Louis-Joseph, Marquis de Montcalm-Gozon de Saint-Véran. (From a contemporary portrait)

and great happiness. The former Angélique Louise Talon du Boulay bore him ten children, of whom five survived him. In 1741 he fought in Bohemia, and in 1743 became the Colonel of the Régiment d'Auxerrois. Between 1744 and 1746 he saw much hard fighting, including an Italian campaign under Marshal de Maillebois; in 1746 he was captured, after receiving five sabre wounds while rallying his men before the walls of Piacenza. Paroled, he returned to active service in time to be hit by a musket-ball before the Peace of Aix-la-Chapelle in 1748. He was appointed to the American command in February 1756, and promoted major-general on his departure. He was given two battalions as reinforcements. On 3 April 1756, after watching his 1,200 soldiers of the battalions of Royal-Roussillon and La Sarre file aboard ship from the Brest quays, he set sail for New France in the frigate *Licorne*. As second and third in command he had been given Brigadier the Chevalier de Lévis, and Colonel the Chevalier de Bourlamaque, men in whom the better aspects of the eighteenth-century French aristocracy were conspicuous. One of Montcalm's aides, and soon a trusted friend, was a young officer of humble

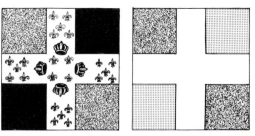

The colours of two of Montcalm's regular regiments – (left) the La Reine, and (right) the Guyenne. That of the La Reine is quartered, first and third green, second and fourth black. A white cross bears gold fleur-de-lis and gold and red crowns. The Guyenne colour is quartered, first and third green, second and fourth pale buff, with a white cross. (R.G.W.)

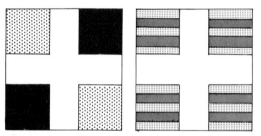

The regimental colours of the La Sarre (left) and Béarn (right). The La Sarre's quarterings are first and third a dark reddish brown, second and fourth black, with a white cross. The Béarn has two scarlet and three pale buff stripes in each quarter, with a white cross. (R.G.W.)

his ambition, he took every opportunity to slander the general and his regular troops, while inventing triumphs for his own brutal militia and sometimes less than impressive colony troops. He hotly resisted attempts to place all categories of troops under Montcalm, thus adding the complication of a split command. It was not a happy atmosphere in which the new General had to assess his task.

His forces were not numerous considering the prospect which faced them, of increasingly heavy British attacks on vital points in the French line. That 'line' itself was misleading, of course. There was no connected system, merely a series of forts, blockhouses, stockaded settlements, missions, and Indian villages stretching, at intervals of many miles, across a howling wilderness of thick forest, swamp, rivers, and lakes. Infiltration was relatively simple for forest-trained men, of whom the British provincials were beginning to find large numbers. Travel was by canoe and light *bateau*, for the waterways were the only practical highways. The game was not very plentiful in many areas, and in winter particularly the isolated posts, their gardens frozen over and the woods silent, relied on staple supplies like grain and salted fish to survive. Troops usually suffered ten or twenty per cent casualties from disease at any one time, due to primitive facilities and total ignorance of hygiene.

Montcalm's little army numbered perhaps 2,500 effectives of the *troupes de terre*, the regulars from Old France, with certain local elements. The regiments of La Reine, Languedoc, Guyenne and Béarn had each provided a battalion for Dieskau's expeditionary force. (A French infantry battalion at that time numbered about 500 men, in one grenadier, one light, and eight fusilier companies each mustering one captain, one lieutenant, one ensign, one or two cadets, two sergeants, two corporals, a drummer, and about forty-five men.) With Montcalm had come battalions of the regiments of Royal-Roussillon and La Sarre, more than 300 of whom were now laid low by sickness. (The Royal-Roussillon was an old regiment; it had originally been raised by Cardinal Mazarin in about 1657 in the regions of Roussillon and Catalonia, with the title *Catalan-Mazarin*. It had adopted the new title on being taken on the royal establishment in 1667.) In addition to the infantry

birth named Bougainville; later in life a famous navigator, he was, happily, a prolific writer of journals. With all these officers Montcalm quickly established friendly relations based on genuine mutual regard.

Such a relationship with his new chief, Governor-General Vaudreuil, was to prove beyond his grasp. Trouble was brewing even before he presented himself at Montreal in May 1756. He was ever tactful, but the two men would be thrown into conflict (and eventually bitter hostility) by forces they could not control. Vaudreuil, colony-born, distrusted men sent out from France and resented the necessity of having regular troops in Canada, especially troops only nominally under his orders. An egoist whose talents did not match

Montcalm had small numbers of engineer and artillery specialists.

The main local force was the colonial *gendarmerie*, the independent companies of the *Compagnies Franches de la Marine*. (All French colonies came under the Minister of Marine, and the anchor was the badge of French colonial infantry until the 1960s.) This service had been created out of an earlier organization in the 1690s, and provided the only uniformed French presence in America until Dieskau's arrival in 1755. For most of the first half of the eighteenth century there were only about 800 men – some twenty-eight companies of thirty or so men each. By 1750 the strength had risen to thirty companies of fifty men; in 1756 it went up to thirty of sixty-five, and in 1757 it would rise again to forty companies of sixty-five. Officers and men were recruited in France, and encouraged to settle in the colony on completion of eight years' service. (As the war dragged on and

'Ready your arms!' as performed by men in the second and third ranks of the French infantry line.

manpower became more of a problem, local men were accepted into the *Compagnies Franches*. A proportion of the officers had, in practice, been drawn from the local *noblesse* for many years.) In peacetime some units looked more like settlers than soldiers, even before discharge. The companies were scattered as garrisons and escorts all over the frontiers of the settled areas, often far out in the wilds. There was little to do of a military nature, and before Governor Duquesne tightened discipline it appears that many of the officers were mostly concerned with fur-trading. The colony troops were tough and hardy forest-fighters, but unsophisticated by European standards. They were unreliable in pitched battles on open ground – but such battles scarcely ever occurred. Some of the officers and men of the more isolated commands 'went native', and adopted certain aspects of Indian customs which did not endear them to the regular troops, who considered them, at best, provincial. Although there was a total of some 1,850 men on the establishment, they were answerable primarily to the Governor, and were not always placed at Montcalm's disposal, although some companies took part in virtually every one of the frontier battles. In 1758 there were twenty-four companies on detached service in Louisbourg, reducing the Canadian force to about 1,000.

The third category of troops was the Canadian militia. This was organized by Governor Frontenac in 1672. Each parish had to provide a company of men according to a quota system designed to leave enough men at liberty to keep agriculture and trade going. Every able-bodied man between the ages of fifteen and sixty was eligible, and in theory Vaudreuil had 15,000 men at his beck and call. In fact it was undesirable to call so many from the plough, and even in 1758 only about 1,100 were actually called to arms – although about 4,000 were employed in transporting and supplying the troops, a job at which they were skilled and reliable. When mustered they received no pay, but were given arms and ammunition, and could buy the musket at cost and take it home when disbanded – a considerable inducement.

Ever boastful of their prowess and ever contemptuous of the blundering of the regulars in the forest-fighting of the early war years, the militia had a mixed reputation. Discipline was not good, and some of the wilder elements were little better than the Indians – they certainly took scalps on occasion. They were tough and woodscrafty, and achieved some notable coups when accompanying Indians on raiding parties; but against formed regular troops they were most unreliable and apt to break and run at the first volley.

For scouting and patrol work Montcalm relied on the *coureurs de bois* and the tribes themselves. The former were the backwoodsmen, the trappers and hunters who in peacetime lived in the forest, alone or with the Indians, only coming into the settlements once or twice a year to trade for necessities. They were persecuted in peacetime, as 'drop-outs' from the tightly ordered feudal hierarchy of New France, but in wartime their fieldcraft and knowledge of the forest trails were invaluable. The war-parties which played such red havoc with settlements along the fringe of the British colonies usually consisted of Indians, a few of these 'woods-runners', forty or fifty militiamen, and a handful of colony troops, led by crafty partisan leaders like Marin and Langlade, with two or three high-spirited young *chevaliers* along for experience, painted and feathered like Indians. These bushrangers were often as ruthless as the Indians, and their scalp-taking was only the least of the horrors they either committed, or watched indifferently.

The Indians themselves, as Montcalm quickly found, were not to be included in any plan of campaign. They were extremely capricious and unreliable, and tended to come and go as they pleased. They demanded endless hand-outs, and were chiefly useful as scouts when the enemy was of any strength. They never repeated their performance at Braddock's Massacre. Montcalm found them repulsive and infuriating. '. . . One needs the patience of an angel to get on with them. Ever since I have been here, I have had nothing but visits, harangues, and deputations of these gentry. . . . They make war with astounding cruelty, sparing neither men, women nor children. . .'. The Marquis spared his lady the information that they were also cannibals. The least unreliable were generally the 'Christian' Indians from the missions of Canada – the Hurons of Lorette, the Abenakis from St Francis and Batiscan, the Iroquois of Caughnawaga and L. Présentation, and the Iroquois and Algonquins c the Two Mountains on the Ottawa.

While he got to know his men and his surround ings, Montcalm was exercised by rumours that th British would renew their attempts agains Ticonderoga and Crown Point, and Fort Niagar and Fort Frontenac on Lake Ontario. He im proved the hour by having more substantial forti fications prepared, particularly at Niagara where he sent the Béarn – and at Ticonderoga. A the latter place he ordered the construction of strong fort, to be named Carillon. It was one c the most strategic positions in America; it com manded the most constricted point of the series c waterways which sprung from the heart of Canada and pointed like a highroad at the heart of th northern colonies of Great Britain.

Oswego

By June 1756 the Béarn was camped at the now strong Fort Niagara; the La Sarre and Guyenne with militia support, guarded Fort Frontenac; La Reine and Languedoc were at Ticonderoga, and the remaining battalion was in reserve at Montreal A scare that month, prompted by an Indian repor that 10,000 British were marching on Ticonderoga took Montcalm· to that important post with th Royal-Roussillon, detachments of the *Compagnie Franches*, and some militia. The rumour prove false; the provincials were indeed moving mer and supplies up the line from the Hudson and Mohawk to the forward posts at Fort Edward and Fort William Henry (the new post at the tip o Lake George, near the site of Johnson's camp and battlefield), and red-coated regulars were arrivin in the Thirteen Colonies, but there was n immediate danger. The colonies were performing their usual ritual dance, and the usual ill-feeling between provincial and regular soldiers wa reaping its usual harvest of inefficiency and bloody-mindedness at every level of organization. Montcalm was well satisfied by what he saw at Ticonderoga, and gave command of the new Fort Carillon to his gallant and courtly deputy, de Lévis. The fort was a sturdy redoubt with four bastions, stone barracks, bombproof shelters, and outworks blasted in some places from the solid rock.

Throughout the summer of 1756 the provincials moved men and supplies up to Oswego on Lake Ontario, and Fort William Henry on Lake George, and the convoys of pack-horses and *bateaux* provided targets too tempting for the Indian and French raiding parties to pass up. The woods were alive with them, but they did not have things all their own way. One Robert Rogers, a provincial officer of originality, skill and ruthlessness, was already making a name for his 'Rangers' with daring reconnaissance patrols deep in French territory.

One of the main anxieties of the British was Oswego, the foothold on Lake Ontario, between the two French posts at Frontenac on the north shore and Niagara on the south. It was a vital base for operations against these two positions, and the winter had left it in a deplorable state. When Shirley had retreated the previous autumn he had left it garrisoned by 700 provincials, but now it held not half this number of scarecrows. Decimated by disease, hunger, and cold during the harsh winter, they could hardly stand guard without crutches. The spring had seen drafts of raw recruits moved hurriedly up to reinforce

One of the movements of the 'Ground arms!' – showing how the soldier holds his decorated grenadier pouch with his left arm behind his back. Note the tightly queued hair.

them, but this was a mere palliative. Early in August Lord Loudon, the new British Commander-in Chief, sent Colonel Webb up from Albany with the rebuilt 44th Foot, but while still on the road they met fleeing boatmen who told a startling tale.

Persistent rumours during July of British moves against Fort Carillon had prompted Montcalm and Vaudreuil to adopt a new plan. They would launch an attack on Oswego, long a cherished project of the Governor's; it would be intended mainly as a feint to draw troops off from the southern end of Lake George, but if it seemed to prosper it could always be reinforced. Leaving Ticonderoga in the hands of de Lévis and a force of 3,000 men, Montcalm reached Fort Frontenac on 29 July 1756, where he mustered his expedition. The La Sarre and Guyenne were already at the fort, and the Béarn soon arrived from Niagara. A detachment of the colony troops, some militia, and about 250 savages brought the total strength to about 3,000 men, with plentiful artillery – some of it captured in Braddock's Massacre. Supported by some eighty gunboats, Montcalm's force crossed the lake under cover of darkness, and by 8 August the whole army was concealed at Niaouré Bay. On the 9th an advance party began a march along the shore under cover of the forest, to cover the landing of the rest who followed by boat. At midnight on 10 August the landing was made without opposition about a mile and a half from Oswego. The next day the attack began on Fort Ontario.

Oswego consisted of three forts: Fort Ontario, a new star-shaped timber fort on the right bank of the river where it entered Lake Ontario; Old Fort Oswego, opposite it on the other bank of the river; and nearby an unfinished stockade known as 'Fort Rascal' for its general lack of amenities, once a cattle-pen but now sketchily fortified by 150 New Jersey provincials. It was clear to Colonel Mercer, the Oswego commandant based in the Old Fort, that Fort Ontario could never withstand the cannon he saw being dragged into position, despite its own small battery of swivels and mortars. After a day of harassment from cover by the swarming Canadians and Indians, the garrison of Fort Ontario (some 370 provincials of Pepperell's Regiment) were signalled and ordered to join their comrades in Old Fort Oswego. They spiked their battery and rowed across the river to the other fort. This had roughly-built clay and stone walls and a stone trading post in the centre of the compound; but again, nothing that could withstand a twelve-pound cannon-ball at close range. Old Fort Oswego was held by Shirley's Regiment mostly raw recruits and invalids, joined now by the other garrison and a few boatmen and waggoners. In all, including some hundred or so women who disturbed the air with their wailing at the prospect of Indian massacre, there were perhaps 1,500 souls in Colonel Mercer's care.

By the morning of 14 August some twenty cannon had been set up by Montcalm's soldiers on the hillock on which Fort Ontario stood, and these opened a brisk fire which quickly breached the walls of Old Fort Oswego in a score of places – though not without loss to the gun crews from the defenders. The defences of Old Fort Oswego were almost non-existent on the east, where stood the sister fort now in the enemy's hands, and all the cannon pointed west. These were manhandled over to the east and installed in pork-barrel casemates. Despite this spirited performance, Mercer knew his command was doomed; it was isolated, outnumbered, outgunned, and man for man it was in a sorry state compared to Montcalm's tough regulars and howling savages. When the gallant Mercer himself was cut in half by a cannon-ball, the white flag was not long in fluttering up. The garrison was in no position to haggle about terms, with the Indians swarming round the walls under the tenuous control of the French *chevaliers*. When the gates were opened the Indians and scarcely more civilized Canadians flooded in, plundering and jostling, and quickly drinking themselves stupid on captured rum. Some prisoners tried to run, and were tomahawked on the spot; many others would have perished, had not Montcalm rushed from group to group, offering the chiefs extravagant cash presents to forgo their bloody sport. Eventually the expedition marched for home, loaded with prisoners and booty, and leaving behind a burning fort, stripped of its artillery and such provisions as could be carried. The English casualties had not reached fifty, and the French had even fewer; yet the position of the Thirteen Colonies was once more endangered, and French troops (as opposed to

Indians) had won their most important battle yet on American soil. Now that there was no enemy assembly-point on the lake from which attacks could be prepared and launched, relatively modest French garrisons could hold Frontenac and Niagara, allowing the rest of the field army to be gathered to Fort Carillon. Perhaps they might even seize Albany, centre of the Dutch fur-traders? It was a heady return march.

The failure of the British provincials to achieve any worthwhile military objective in 1756 was partly due to weaknesses peculiar to them. Without a military establishment, disunited, discordant, and frugal, they had the greatest difficulty in building an army early enough in the campaigning season to set afoot any major operation. The growing activity of New England raiding-parties in the summer and autumn of 1756, such as those led with such dash by the famous Rogers, stemmed from the particular strengths of the provincials: their individual hardiness and resource, and their skill in 'commando' operations as distinct from manœuvres involving large formed units.

As the winter of 1756–7 set in, Montcalm concentrated at Fort Carillon an army of 5,300 regulars and Canadians. The enemy Commander-in-Chief, Lord Loudon, was at Fort Edward; in all he had some 10,000 provincial and regular troops, scattered throughout the frontier regions. Neither general wished to mount any large-scale operations for the time being, and as the winter grew harder they relied upon patrols and raids to keep the war going. The frontiers of the Thirteen Colonies were now guarded, sketchily, by a series of blockhouses and small forts of widely varying quality, a judgment equally applicable to the garrisons. In late 1756 the Indians raged virtually unchecked, and scalp-hunting for bounty was the order of the day. (One of Governor Vaudreuil's least attractive traits, in modern eyes, was his meticulous chronicling of every British settler's scalp turned in to his agents; the records have an undertone of satisfaction which is faintly repulsive.) The partisan warfare, which took the form of a deadly game of hide-and-seek through the silent woods around Fort Carillon, Fort William Henry and other posts on Lake George, was often enlivened by daring raids on French posts and Indian villages by parties of provincial

Two contemporary drawings of curious but compelling style, showing 'an Indian pursuing a wounded enemy with his Tomahawk' and 'an Indian dress'd for War, with a Scalp'. (Courtauld Institute)

raiders. These operations, which sometimes took small parties deep into French Canada, wreaked havoc on the nerves of outlying garrisons, and Rogers's Rangers acquired an awesome reputation. The British had few client Indians and were forced to rely on these ruthless and increasingly confident backwoodsmen, who in consequence became very experienced and skilled. The French

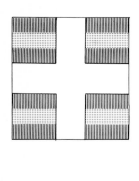

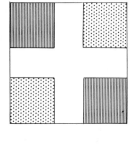

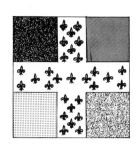

Colours of (top) the Berry and (centre) the Languedoc regiments. Berry had a white cross with two violet and one pale buff stripe in each quarter. The white cross of the Languedoc is surrounded by first and third quarters in violet, second and fourth in dark brown. (lower) The colours of the Régiment de Royal-Roussillon: a white cross with golden fleur-de-lis, with quarterings of dark blue, scarlet, green, and pale buff. (R.G.W.)

Thirteen Colonies – which complained bitterly about billeting British regulars during the winter.

In March 1757 an unsuccessful expedition was mounted against Fort William Henry; Montcalm helped with the planning, but it was very much Vaudreuil's project and was commanded by his brother, Rigaud. A force of 1,600 men of the militia, the raiders, the *Compagnies Franches*, and one or two friendly tribes crept down the lake and attacked at night from the ice. The assault was botched; after indecisive manœuvres and a couple of days of harassing fire the attackers retreated again, having succeeded in burning some outbuildings and some boats laid up on shore by the fort.

Fort William Henry

The campaigning season of 1757 opened at a time of increasingly bitter factional feeling in New France. While diplomatic to his face, Vaudreuil lost no opportunity to slander Montcalm secretly. No matter how much he resented the regulars' presence in his satrapy, however, Vaudreuil was forced to concede that a reinforcement was necessary in view of the build-up of regular strength by the enemy. His request was granted, and two battalions of the Régiment de Berry arrived at Quebec in the spring and summer – the Second in April, the Third in July.

No immediate offensive was possible; a large British fleet was known to be outfitting for America in English ports, and if its target was Quebec then the regulars must stay in the heart of the colony. In fact the invasion force was destined for Louisbourg, the great fortress on the rocky Nova Scotia seaboard. It anchored at Halifax early in July, and was joined by most of Lord Loudon's

war-parties were made up of Indians and *coureurs de bois*, led by such formidable partisans as the famous Marin. As much as sheer vengeance, these raids were intended to secure prisoners, a vital part of the information-gathering of both sides; and to disrupt the supply convoys, both of overland sledges and of canoes and river-boats, upon which the isolated forts of both sides relied.

In the depth of winter the French army was pulled back from Ticonderoga to the Montreal area where Montcalm and his staff wintered; the fort was left guarded by five or six companies of regulars. At Fort William Henry, Major Eyre kept watch with 400 redcoats, and the tattered provincial units, most of them at the end of their specified period of service, moved back to the best regular units, thus leaving the western frontier dangerously weak. Indecision and confusion, conflicting orders and poor intelligence plagued the expedition, and in the end no assault was made on Louisbourg; but while Loudon's redcoats idled around Halifax, Montcalm struck. He took Fort William Henry.

In July 1757 a great army was gathered at Ticonderoga. For months the French agents had been busy collecting food to feed 12,000 men for a month. Since May Bourlamaque had been camped at Fort Carillon with the Béarn and the Royal-Roussillon, setting all in order after the winter and sending patrols down the lake to watch the British. For months Montcalm and his officers had been visiting Indian villages, to sing with them the war-song. Now the Chevalier de Lévis had a large tented camp near the Ticonderoga sawmill, in which the La Sarre, the La Reine, the Languedoc, and the Guyenne awaited their orders. Other camps contained thousands of men of the *Compagnies Franches*, the militia, and the Mission Indians, while the fires of the wild tribes smoked all around: nearly 2,000 of them, of forty-one tribes and sub-tribes. The major distinction between the Mission Indians and their wild brothers seems to have been that the former had guns in place of the bows and spears of the latter, and had been persuaded by their priests to give up cannibalism on all but the most special occasions. The officers from Old France were shocked by the treatment of the prisoners which scouting parties brought in almost every day, and used to buy them from the Indians to save their lives whenever they could. Uncontrollable and infuriating though the tribesmen were, it was sadly true that, in Bougainville's words, ' . . . here in the forests of America we can no more do without them than cavalry on the plains'.

The army was to move partly by land, partly by water, and numbers of *bateaux* had been prepared; the artillery, numbering more than thirty cannon and half as many mortars, was mounted on platforms built across two *bateaux* lashed together. On 30 July 1757 de Lévis took to the woods with about 2,500 men; and on 1 August Montcalm embarked with about 5,000 more, leaving 400 at Fort Carillon. Of the total of about 7,600 in his

Baudouin engraving of an officer of the Grenadiers de la Garde Françoises (*sic*) carrying a fusil in the regulation position.

army about 1,600 were Indians. The French flotilla must have made an impressive sight as it slipped over the water close to the wooded shores of the lake. First came a cloud of birch-bark canoes filled with painted savages. Then came the flat-bottomed *bateaux*, under sail or oars, more than 250 of them, filled with drab militia and brightly uniformed regulars of the La Reine, Languedoc, La Sarre, and Guyenne. Next came the cannon and mortars on their makeshift barges, rowed by the militia of Saint-Ours, and followed by the white coats of the Béarn and the Royal-Roussillon, the provision boats, the hospital boats, and boat-load after boat-load of Canadians.

A French soldier in winter campaign dress, 1755–60. There was little major movement of troops in the harsh Canadian winter, as the logistic problems of simply sitting out the winter safely in one of the isolated forts were enormous. This soldier carries extra powder in a horn, and a hatchet for hand-to-hand fighting. He wears a capote or blanket-coat and locally-made mittens, and his musket is muffled with rag to protect the priming from damp. (G. A. Embleton, courtesy *Tradition*)

The main force rendezvoused successfully with de Levis's advance party; and on 3 August the first clash took place, as the scouting parties closed in on the British fort, and the defenders sallied out to drive in their cattle and burn their outhouses to clear fields of fire. Fort William Henry was an irregular bastioned square of logs and rammed earth protected to the north by the lake, to the east by swamps, and to the south and west by ditches and small outworks. The road south to Fort Edward, fourteen miles away, lay on the east beyond the swamp, covered by an entrenched position on a hill beyond it. The fort was commanded by the gallant Lieutenant-Colonel Monro of the 35th Foot; he had at his disposal seventeen cannon, and several mortars and swivels. His garrison numbered 2,200, more than half of them provincials. At Fort Edward lay General Webb, in an unenviable position. He had only about 1,600 men, largely provincials; another 800 or so guarded forts on the road to Albany. He could not respond to the messages which Monro sent him, requesting immediate reinforcement, without leaving the route to Albany naked to the invader. His available force was too small to risk on the forest road, haunted as it was by Indians, and would only reduce the odds to about two to one even if it could reach the beleaguered fort. Nevertheless, one is tempted to believe that if the positions had been reversed, Monro would have tried it. Webb stayed where he was, sending frantic appeals for militia to the Thirteen Colonies, militia which could never arrive in time. In answer to Monro's repeated messages he finally sent word that surrender on decent terms, if obtainable, was the best plan. His letter was brought to Montcalm by the Indians who butchered Webb's messenger in the woods.

If Webb was haunted by Braddock's ghost, then Montcalm was not free of memories of Dieskau's ruin so close to his present camp. There was to be no frontal assault; he had the men, the guns, and the time for a formal eighteenth-century siege. While his red men and irregulars surrounded the area and cut off all escape, his regulars dug parallels, and set up batteries. As each cannon was landed and emplaced it opened fire, and for days the fort and the trenches exchanged a brisk

Print of nineteenth-century vintage purporting to show Montcalm trying to save the victims of the Indian massacre after the surrender of Fort William Henry in 1757. (P. H. Gidaly)

bombardment. The Indians were delighted with the show, and tended to lounge around in eager anticipation of the fall of the fort. Montcalm had warned Monro to surrender at the outset, as the tribes would be difficult to restrain if frustrated by a long defence; Monro, as honour bound, had refused. After a few days, Montcalm sent young Bougainville into the fort under flag of truce, with Webb's captured letter, urging surrender once more. Again it was refused, in the most courteous terms.

By the morning of 9 August, however, a different mood prevailed, and Monro sent his emissaries into the French camp. More than 300 of the defenders had been killed and wounded, and many others lay helpless in the grip of the smallpox which was raging in the fort. The ramparts had been breached in several places, and nearly all the cannon had either burst or been knocked out by French fire. An assault, if pressed, could not be repulsed; and Monro now asked for terms.

It was agreed that the garrison would march out with the honours of war, keeping one of their surviving cannon as a gesture of respect for their gallant defence, and would be escorted to Fort Edward by a French detachment; there were other terms connected with paroles and exchanges of prisoners. Before agreeing to these terms Montcalm specifically consulted the Indian chiefs, asking their consent, and their assurance that they could and would restrain their warriors. They consented to everything, and reassured him on every point. The garrison then evacuated the fort and marched to join their comrades in the entrenched camp, which had also held out, and which was included in the surrender. Immediately the Indians swarmed into the fort and butchered the bedridden sick who still lay within. They then turned on the entrenched camp, accompanied by some of the wilder Canadians. They roamed through the camp, plundering what they fancied, and threatening the uneasy captives, who had

21

many women and children among them. The French guard seem to have been unable or unwilling to keep them out.

When Montcalm heard of this he ran to the camp in person, and seems to have used every device to persuade the chiefs to restrain their men. After an afternoon of frantic diplomacy, with the threat of massacre a hair's breadth away, he seems to have restored some order and even secured a promise of representatives of each tribe to accompany the prisoners on the march to Fort Edward as guarantees of good faith. His efforts were, in the long run, unavailing. Some more of the wounded were murdered during the night, and shortly after the dismal march began the next day, the Indians who were crowding round the forlorn column raised a whoop, and fell on them. The escort's part in the affair seems discreditable, though not so much so as that of many Canadian militiamen and officers, who watched fifty white men, women, and children butchered before their eyes with the most callous disinterest. About 200 of the prisoners were dragged into the forest and never seen again. Montcalm and his officers, hurrying to the scene, tried to restrain the savages physically, at risk of their lives, and eventually provided a proper escort to take the shocked survivors to Fort Edward. One finds it hard to feel sympathy for the Indians who later contracted smallpox from the corpses they scalped so eagerly, and died in great numbers.

Louisbourg and Fort Carillon

The capture, and subsequent burning, of Fort William Henry was the only major French operation of 1757. When the news reached the Thirteen Colonies there was great alarm, and some declared

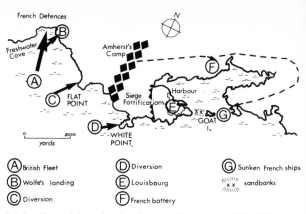

Main dispositions in the siege and capture of Louisbourg, by a British army under General Amherst, in the summer of 1758. (R.G.W.)

New York itself in danger; but Montcalm, without the means to move his artillery swiftly to Fort Edward and in the expectation of heavy British reinforcements (which did, in fact, arrive soon afterwards), returned to Ticonderoga. He spent the winter of 1757–8 in Quebec and Montreal, on bad terms with Vaudreuil and writing wry letters to his friends. The colony, as a whole, had a bad winter. Food was scarce, and the consequent riots by civilians infected the *Compagnies Franches*, and even the regulars of the Béarn. The Chevalier de Lévis quelled the trouble with some forceful but nicely judged language. Around Lake George the partisans of both sides stalked through the snow-covered forests; the redoubtable Rogers butchered French beefs under the very walls of Fort Carillon, and left cavalier notes fixed to their horns. His sense of humour was blunted in March 1758, however, by a savage fight with a French party which cost him 125 men, and nearly his life.

In London the winter saw William Pitt take over the helm of government, with a consequent improvement in the direction of the war. Pitt's three priority targets were Louisbourg, to clear a naval road for an attack on Quebec; Fort Carillon, to remove the festering sore in the flank of the northern colonies; and Fort Duquesne, to break the enemy grip on the Ohio Valley. While Montcalm wrote loving messages to his family, and exchanged dryly humorous notes with his staff officers, his fate was being sealed across the Atlantic. Lord Loudon was recalled, and his second, Major-General Abercrombie, took his place by right of seniority; but Pitt actually hoped

The *justaucorps* of three regiments which, with the *Volontaires Étrangers*, formed the main garrison of Louisbourg in 1758. (Left) Bourgogne: coat entirely white, three buttons on pocket and cuff, waistcoat red, buttons and lace gold. (Centre) Artois: coat entirely white, nine buttons on pocket and six on cuff, waistcoat red, buttons and lace gold. (Right) Cambis: red collar, cuffs and waistcoat, three buttons on pocket and cuff in sequence silver-gold-silver, hat lace mixed gold and silver. (G. A. Embleton)

that Brigadier Lord Howe of the 55th Foot, 'the best soldier in the British Army', would be the moving spirit behind the planned expedition to Fort Carillon. Louisburg was to be the goal of Major-General Jeffrey Amherst, with a young officer named James Wolfe among his brigadiers; and Fort Duquesne was to be attacked by Brigadier John Forbes. Among the reinforcements sent across the Atlantic were two regiments of the Highland troops which Pitt had had a hand in raising years before.

British troops under Amherst landed on Île Royale on 8 June 1758, and the fortress of Louisbourg came under siege shortly thereafter. With a mile and a half of stone ramparts, four great bastions, nearly 250 artillery pieces and a garrison of more than 3,000 regulars, Louisbourg was the most formidable fortress on the continent. When it surrendered on 26 July the walls on the landward side were breached and two of the bastions crumbling; not a single cannon was left in working order on that face; the town within the walls was almost entirely destroyed by the British bombardment; and a quarter of the garrison were casualties. The stout Drucour and his men of the battalions of Artois, Bourgogne, Cambis, and *Volontaires Étrangers*, and the *Compagnies Franches de la Marine*, were ready to fight on, but were prevailed upon to surrender to save the inhabitants further suffering. The aftermath of Fort William Henry lay heavy on French consciences – if not on Vaudreuil's, then on those of Frenchmen nearer

Artist's impression of General Abercrombie supervising the embarkation of his army on Lake George for the attack on Fort Carillon in September 1758. (P. H. Gidaly)

the sound of gunfire – and there was a certain unwillingness to force the enemy to storm the breach. Historically, this gave the attackers the unquestioned right to sack the town once it fell into their hands.

At every stage young Brigadier Wolfe distinguished himself. He led the real invasion party ashore in Freshwater Cove, while Lawrence and Whitmore led diversions against Flat Point and White Point. He marched his brigade round the harbour and set up a battery on Lighthouse Point, silencing the French guns on Goat Island. He was always to the fore in the savage clashes between besiegers, sally-parties, and harassing militia.

Although Quebec now lay open to him, it was well on in the season, and Amherst ignored the temptation and sailed to join Abercrombie at Lake George with six regiments. Montcalm now faced a probable assault on Fort Carillon by overwhelming numbers, and faced it without the colony troops or militia; Vaudreuil, whose spite had reached the point where he could risk damaging his King's cause if he could ruin Mont-

calm thereby, had drawn them, and the stalwart de Lévis, off to Montreal for some scheme of his own. Reports from a prisoner in mid-June, of '30,000 British' coming to Fort Carillon within a fortnight, forced the Governor to release de Lévis and promise reinforcements, but there was no reason to hope that either would arrive in time. Montcalm seems to have been through a period of indecision. He spread his little army of regulars along the probable line of British advance, with detachments at the landing-places at the head of Lake George, the end of the portage track, the sawmill by the narrows west of the fort, and the fort itself – where the Second Berry was set to digging the beginnings of a line of outworks half a mile in front of the fort. He kept his options open as to the point where he would stand and fight. His prospects were hardly encouraging.

Abercrombie embarked on 5 July from his camp at the southern end of Lake George – surely a haunted camp-ground if ever one existed. His army numbered about 15,000. Some 6,000 were regulars of the 27th, 44th, 46th, 55th, and

Major-General the Marquis of Montcalm

A

1 Canadian militiaman, Trois Rivières
  Brigade 1759
2 Fusilier, Compagnies Franches de la
  Marine, *c.* 1750
3 Fusilier, Swiss Regiment 'Karrer',
  Louisbourg, 1745

1

2

3

B

MICHAEL ROFFE

1 **Fusilier, Compagnies Franches, winter campaign dress, 1750s**
2 **Fusilier, Compagnies Franches, summer fatigue dress, 1750s**
3 **Coureur de bois, 1750s**

MICHAEL ROFFE

C

1 Fusilier, Régiment de Béarn,
  1755–60
2 Grenadier, Régiment de La
  Reine, with battalion colour:
  1755–60
3 Officer, Corps of Engineers,
  1750s

1 **Sergeant, Régiment de Royal-Roussillon, 1756–60**
2 **Corporal, Régiment de Guyenne, marching order, 1755–60**
3 **Mission Indian, 1750s**

MICHAEL ROFFE

E

1 Corporal, Régiment de La Sarre, off-duty dress, 1756–60
2 Company officer, Régiment de Berry, Quebec, 1757
3 Fusilier, Régiment de La Reine, summer campaign dress, 1758

MICHAEL ROFF

1 Drummer, Régiment de Guyenne, 1755–60
2 Company officer, Régiment de Languedoc, summer campaign dress, 1758
3 Woods Indian warrior, 1750s

MICHAEL ROFFE

G

1 **Cadet-Gentilhomme, Corps Royal d'Artillerie, 1757**
2 **Grenadier, Régiment de Cambis, Louisbourg, 1755**
3 **Grenadier, Régiment de Languedoc, 1755–60**

H

MICHAEL ROFFE

Both Foot, the 42nd Highlanders and the 60th Royal Americans, with detachments of Light Infantry under Gage. There were about 9,000 provincials, with Massachusetts well to the fore, and Rogers scouted ahead with his green-coated Rangers. Abercrombie himself was an undistinguished commander, a man of connection rather than talent. The heart and brain of the army was the gay, brilliant young Brigadier Lord Howe, a thirty-four-year-old officer who seems to have made a remarkable impression on all who met him. He was loved and respected by all ranks, not least because he unfailingly shared every hardship of the common soldiers. He performed marvels of diplomacy to reconcile the mutually resentful regular and provincial officers; and he spared no effort in his determination to fit himself and his army for forest campaigning, whether they liked it or not.

The British army sailed up to Lake George in a convoy of canoes, whale-boats, and barges six miles long, and landed, complete with artillery, by noon on 6 July. It was planned to sweep north round the outside of the narrows between the lakes, turning east and south again to approach Ticonderoga from the landward side. Late that afternoon the head of Howe's column, pushing north through thick woodland, blundered into a strong French party which was trying to regain the shelter of the fort. In a confused skirmish Lord Howe was shot dead, and gloom settled on the entire army. Pitt had wanted him to be the moving spirit – but now the spirit was quenched. Abercrombie wasted a day in indecisive countermarching, pulling the troops back to the landings and then deciding to advance by means of the portage track anyhow. Montcalm, who had camped near the sawmill with his main force until the evening of the 6th, now fell back on the fort itself and made use of the precious day the enemy general had given him.

Throughout the 7th, officers and men of the battalions of Old France sweated and heaved side by side, and a nine-foot wall of logs, loop-holed for defenders and zigzagging to give enfilading fire, rose in front of the fort. It was strengthened with sacks and baskets of earth at some points; and in front a 'killing-ground' was provided. A thick, tangled abatis of felled trees was spread over the open ground, their branches interwoven and

Baudouin plate showing an officer – apparently a senior officer – with an espontoon.

25

Baudouin plate showing first, second and third ranks of the battle line at the 'Aim' position.

pointed in a terrible obstacle, as bad as a barbed-wire entanglement. Despite the prodigies his men performed, Montcalm had little cause for optimism as dawn rose on the 8th. With rations for eight days, he stood every chance of being cut off from all help. He had been cheered by the last-minute arrival of de Lévis during the night, with 400 regulars, but this still only brought his strength up to 3,600, against 15,000 enemy. Had Abercrombie chosen any one of numerous plans of attack based on steadily closing in around Ticonderoga and bringing his artillery up from Lake George to pound the fort into splinters, disaster was inevitable. As it happened Abercrombie did the one thing Montcalm had no right to hope for – he sent waves of infantry against the French defences, without support.

When the French pickets were driven in by the advancing Rangers at about noon, and the red coats began to show between the trees at the far edge of the clearing, Montcalm was ready. On the earthwork wall, half a mile in front of the fort, the regulars were drawn up. (The wall did not extend as far as the water at each end – the gaps were plugged by Canadians and some ten companies of the *Compagnies Franches*, supported by the cannons of the fort.) The left, or south end, was commanded by Bourlamaque, the centre by Montcalm, and the north or right flank by de Lévis. Bourlamaque had under his command the

La Sarre and Languedoc, under Lieutenant Colonels de Sennezergues and de Privas. In the centre were the Royal-Roussillon and the Third Berry, under de Bernetz and de Trecesson respectively. The La Reine (Lieutenant-Colonel de Roquemarre), the Béarn (Lieutenant-Colonel de L'Hôpital) and the Guyenne (Lieutenant-Colonel de Fonbonne) were on the right. The grenadiers had been detached from all these battalions, and were stationed together as a reserve force about half-way between earthwork and fort. In the fort itself the Second Berry of Lieutenant-Colonel de Trevis kept guard.

Against these experienced soldiers, firing through loop-holes in a wall higher than their heads, Abercrombie launched his infantry with orders to take the position with the bayonet. The first wave struggled for a full hour in the bullet-swept hell of the abatis before falling back exhausted. Gallantly supported by the provincials they hacked their way through the clinging branches with stolid courage, only to fall far from the breastwork, or to die scrabbling at its foot under the terrible cross-fire. They were sent in a second time, clambering now between the bodies of their dead and wounded, which hung in the cruel entanglement as if in some great web; and again the French volleys drove them off, to triumphant shouts of 'Vive le roi' and 'Vive notre général!'

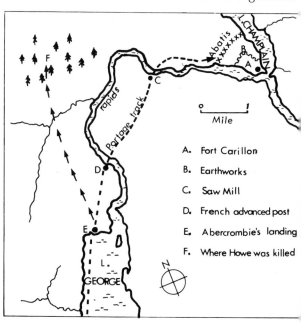

The abortive attack on Fort Carillon, 6–8 September 1758. (R.G.W.)

A. Fort Carillon
B. Earthworks
C. Saw Mill
D. French advanced post
E. Abercrombie's landing
F. Where Howe was killed

from the walls. Montcalm, lost in admiration, recorded seven distinct charges between one and seven o'clock. So many acts of desperate courage were performed that none can be singled out with justice. A few individuals reached the breastwork and hurled themselves at the top, flailing with gun-butt or hatchet, but only a few – and they soon joined the tumbled corpses at the foot of the wall.

The only moment of real danger came with an attack of unequalled determination on the right flank, at about five in the afternoon. This was the famous charge of the Black Watch, when the berserk clansmen hacked their way through the obstacles with their broadswords and actually reached the breastworks. The Guyenne and Béarn were momentarily in difficulties, and Montcalm rushed to the spot with the grenadier reserves. Captain Campbell and his little handful of Highlanders earned the grim honour of being the only British soldiers to die on the French side of the stockade. A flank attack on this column of attackers was led by de Lévis and included some of the colony troops from the extreme flank; they did not distinguish themselves.

As dusk drew on the battle settled into a sporadic musketry duel at long range, to cover the recovery of wounded from the open ground. With twilight came silence, except for the groans of those still crucified in the maze of jagged branches before the walls. Abercrombie had lost 1,944 officers and men killed, wounded, and missing. Montcalm had lost 377. Bourlamaque was badly wounded, Bougainville slightly, and de Lévis had two bullet-holes in his hat. They had stood off an attack of breath-taking courage but little intelligence. They were faced by the certain prospect of more patient assaults, backed by plentiful artillery, now that the first day's losses had taken the fire out of the British infantry. The situation continued to look grim; what reinforcement could they expect from Vaudreuil, and when?

Montcalm's concern was needless. Abercrombie, his intelligence and resolution apparently unequal to the responsibility of command, was retreating with all haste. His army, which still outnumbered the enemy four to one, sailed away down the lake leaving its baggage strewn in its wake. The troops, humiliated and furious at being pulled out without

a chance to avenge the deaths of so many heroic comrades, were soon diminished by dispersal; and the rump of the army dug in on the old site of Fort William Henry, and soon contracted the usual camp diseases. It was a dismal and undeserved end for a proud army, and one which underlined very clearly the fact that leadership is worth more than numbers. The cheering men of the French line battalions ouside Fort Carillon took the point.

The Winter of Despair

The large war-parties, assembled from among the plentiful reinforcements which soon reached Montcalm and went out to harass the British, would, as it transpired, have achieved more of value had they been employed on Lake Ontario. News soon came that, at the end of August 1758, Lieutenant-Colonel Bradstreet and a small army of provincials had made a sudden and successful attack on Fort Frontenac. Although the success was not followed up energetically, command of the lake was thus lost to the French, and a gaping hole opened in their line. Lines of communication between Canada and Fort Duquesne were cut at a time when that post needed all the support possible. In September a force of more than 6,000, made up largely of provincials with a stiffening of Highlanders and Royal Americans, was hacking a new route to the Ohio Valley through the sombre forests of the Alleghenies. It was led by Brigadier John Forbes, a fine Scots officer whose performance in the face of unusually fractious provincials, widespread lack of co-operation, and his own painful illness, was consistently admirable.

His army was not impressive and his problems were legion; yet he pressed on steadily, consolidating his line of advance by setting up fortified

Louis Antoine de Bougainville, Montcalm's aide, chronicler, and friend, and later in his life a famous navigator of the South Seas. (From the Delpech lithograph)

depots, and scouting ahead conscientiously – he had no intention of emulating Braddock. One major blessing was the fact that patient diplomacy, steadfast persistence, and energetic bribery were inducing the Indians of the region to waver in their loyalty to France. Ligneris, commandant at Duquesne, had allowed this vital part of his duties to go by default; and in the early autumn a great treaty was concluded between the tribes and the British under the very noses of the mortified French. Vaudreuil, confident of the tribes' support, had neglected more orthodox precautions. Both the French at Duquesne and the British column in the mountains suffered miserably in the wet autumn weather and the early snows – the French from lack of supplies since the fall of Fort Frontenac, the British from exposure and some dismally mismanaged skirmishes. Yet at the end of November Forbes, wracked and shivering in his litter, had the satisfaction of being carried into the clearing of Fort Duquesne, and seeing the charred ruins of the fort which had started the whole ugly conflict four years previously. Ligneris had blown it up and withdrawn on Presqu'ile and Fort Le Bœuf. Before returning to Pennsylvania – to die

in March – the stalwart Forbes had an outpost established on the site, and gave decent burial at last to the grisly débris of Braddock's column which still littered the forest floor near by.

With Fort Duquesne in the south, Fort Frontenac in the centre, and Louisbourg in the north all lost to them, and the Indian alliance crumbling, the French faced the ruin of the defensive strategy which they had pursued with such success, despite feeble resources, for five years. It was characteristic of Vaudreuil that in his extremity he should hunt for a scapegoat. His slanderous correspondence with France, demanding Montcalm's recall on every pretext from outrageous public utterances to military incompetence, reached a new peak of hysteria. Versailles reminded him with some asperity that he should defer to Montcalm in all things military. Montcalm for his part was driven to despair by the corruption and mismanagement which was in large part responsible for the loss of Fort Duquesne. He wished for nothing better than an honourable recall, and wrote longing letters to Candiac; but he was determined to see his duty out to the end. Even the stolid Canadian population, increasingly uneasy at the evident misgovernment of the colony, began to mutter. Wild inflation, the shortage of every necessity, due to the British blockade of the St Lawrence, and a poor harvest all increased their wretchedness. It seemed that Old France, preoccupied with disasters in Europe, had abandoned her colony to its fate.

In the winter of 1758–9 Bougainville was sent to France to appeal for support. He actually managed to secure an audience with the King – and La Pompadour – but the only gesture they would make was to promote him, Montcalm, de Lévis, and Bourlamaque one rank each. The famous interview between Bougainville and the Colonial Minister, Berryer, is worth repeating. When the Minister answered the young officer's appeal with the cold observation, 'Monsieur, when the house is on fire one cannot occupy oneself with the stable', Bougainville retorted, 'At least, Monsieur, nobody will say that you talk like a horse.' Versailles was adamant, and all that Bougainville could wring from France were a few hundred replacements and a few shiploads of supplies to meet immediate needs. Like Imperial Rome, France was cynically relying on the undeserved devotion of her frontier centurions.

In the spring of 1759 Bougainville returned, bringing firm intelligence that a vast British expedition was bound for Quebec – the figure of 50,000 men was mentioned. Montcalm was ordered to plan his defence with the aim of ensuring, with his tiny resources, that a firm foothold was retained in the heart of Canada, however small. He had a mere 3,500 regular soldiers, about 1,500 colony troops, and a maximum of 13,000 militia to call upon. There was a slim chance that he might make use of geographical advantages to keep the enemy from the area around Quebec and Montreal at least. If he failed, he fully intended to retreat down the entire length of the Mississippi and make a last stand in far-off Louisiana.

Quebec

In June it became certain that Quebec was to be the main target, and almost all the available forces were concentrated in that area; Bourlamaque was left at Ticonderoga with the Second and Third Berry and the La Reine, to guard against an attack in the rear by enemy forces in the Thirteen Colonies. On 26 June 1759 the fleet bearing the British army of Major-General James Wolfe anchored safely off the Isle of Orleans, a few miles from Quebec, and disembarked. Wolfe faced a daunting task. All around him the heights were crowned by French batteries, and nowhere was there a practicable landing-place from which he might advance on Quebec; the great camp of Montcalm was clearly visible on the Beauport Heights. Montcalm naturally hoped to fight a delaying action. If he could prolong the defence, there was a slim chance

that Wolfe might be forced to withdraw by lack of supplies and the approach of winter. Wolfe was impatient to make a decisive move, but bided his time in the knowledge that Amherst was advancing from New England up the great valley which contained Lakes George and Champlain. Bourlamaque could never hold the gate, and Montcalm would be forced to detach more troops.

For a month there were no major operations. Wolfe's army sat on the island and scouted up and down the shores, and Montcalm sat on the heights and watched him. Many of the Canadian militia became bored and discouraged, and deserted in droves. Late in June Wolfe succeeded in seizing Point Levi, opposite the city, and soon established batteries which brought Quebec under fire. The cannon of both sides thundered across the water, the Rangers and Canadians clashed in the thickets, but no major operations seemed to be in train. Even the scouring of the surrounding parishes by Wolfe's light infantry and Highlanders – with occasional disgraceful episodes – failed to tempt Montcalm into leaving his strong position. At the end of July, Wolfe – who now had positions on the north side of the river at the left end of the French encampments – launched a combined land and sea-borne attack on enemy redoubts near the mouth of the Montmorenci. It was beaten off with 450 or so casualties, many of them grenadiers and Royal Americans. The French were cheered by this, and the British depressed. They soon heard news which gave more food for thought. Amherst had taken Fort Carillon on the night of 26 July; it had been abandoned to him, after the blowing of the magazine. This was a wise step, as the precious little army of Bourlamaque could achieve far more in the strong defensive position at Île-aux-Noix at the head of Lake Champlain, where he now dug in. Almost simultaneously, however, the French were suffering another reverse which could not be justified on tactical grounds. A force of about 2,300, regulars and provincials and some hundreds of Indians, commanded by William Johnson after the death of Brigadier Prideaux, scored a double victory. They had besieged Fort Niagara for three weeks when a relief force of 1,300 Canadians, colony troops, and Indians arrived from the French posts on Lake

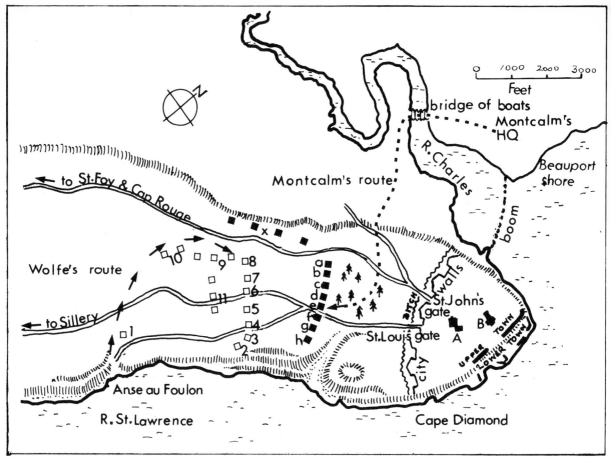

The Battle of the Plains of Abraham. British battle line: (1) Lawrence's Royal Americans, (2) Otway's 35th Foot, (3) Louisbourg Grenadiers, (4) Bragg's 28th Foot, (5) Kennedy's 43rd Foot, (6) Lascelles' 47th Foot, (7) Fraser's 78th Highlanders, (8) Anstruther's 58th Foot, (9) Amherst's 15th Foot, (10) Howe's Light Infantry. (X) indicates Canadian and Indian skirmishers. French battle line: (a) Quebec Militia, (b) Régt. de la Sarre, (c) Régt. de Languedoc, (d) Régt. de Béarn, (e) Régt. de Guyenne, (f) Regt. de Royal-Roussillon, (g) Montreal Militia, (h) Trois Rivières Militia. (A) and (B) in the city itself represent the Ursuline convent and the cathedral. Note that the camps of the French army between June and September 1759 stretched a considerable way along the Beauport shore, beyond the edge of this sketch-map. (R.G.W.)

Erie; this column included many of the hardiest and most dreaded of the partisans and *coureurs de bois*, the 'white Indians'. Johnson promptly split his little force in three; one guarded the trenches before the fort, one guarded the boats by which they had come, and one met and decisively beat the relief force. The fort, under Captain Pouchot of the Béarn, was compelled to surrender. The fleeing partisans burned Presqu'ile, Le Bœuf, and Venango, and fell back on Detroit. The Ohio Valley, Lake Erie, and Lake Ontario were lost for ever.

Dismal as this news was for Montcalm, the campaign season was wearing on and there was still no sign of a British initiative. Bourlamaque was firmly established at Île-aux-Noix with the

Berry and part of the La Reine; and Amherst, instead of marching on Montreal, was indulging his usual passion for fort-building. Wolfe, seriously ill and beginning to despair of his mission, had perhaps 5,000 men available for an attack, once Point Levi and the Isle of Orleans were properly garrisoned. Montcalm had twice that number, counting his dwindling forces of militia, but Wolfe discounted the latter in open battle, even though he had a healthy respect for the regulars. September signalled the imminent close of the season, and Wolfe gambled.

Montcalm, at his headquarters on the Beauport Heights, passed a troubled night on 12/13 September. There was heavy British activity in front of his positions, and he anticipated an attack. There was unusually heavy cannon-fire at several points. He had no fears for the sector up river above the city; the banks were impassable, and anyway his trusted Bougainville was on guard there with 3,000 men – though tired from marching fruitlessly up and down keeping watch on British convoys. As dawn broke he heard cannon above the town, and rode to investigate. As he reached the higher ground near the city he saw, beyond the grey roofs on the narrow grassy plateau of the Plains of Abraham, a line of brick-red. Wolfe had made his famous night climb up the cliffs by the Anse du Foulon, between Bougainville's troops and the city, and now stood ready to meet his enemy face to face at last. There were less than 3,500 men in his battle line, as detachments had to be posted to cover the rear.

Montcalm spurred his horse forward. Behind him the camps came awake, and the troops poured out towards Quebec. The Guyenne was already on the plains, warily standing in the path of the enemy; now the La Sarre, the Languedoc and Béarn, the *Compagnies Franches* and the militia, the proud Royal-Roussillon, all flooded through the narrow streets of Quebec and out of the St Louis and St Jean gates on to the grassy plateau, which rose towards the west, and was dotted with corn-patches and bushes. The British line waited in silence. A light drizzle was falling as Montcalm held council with his staff. All was confusion and contradiction. He had asked Vaudreuil to send after him the men from the camps at the far left of the line along the Beauport shore; these had been promised, but never arrived – the Governor decided to keep them to guard against the chance of another British attack in that sector. The city garrison, also under Vaudreuil's orders, refused to come up, and sent only three of their cannon to Montcalm's field army. While skirmishing parties of Canadians and Indians sniped and worried at the English rear and flanks, and the French regulars sorted themselves into their line, the question of whether to attack or delay was thrashed out. It is said that Montcalm and his staff were unanimously for an attack. It is hard to understand why, and Montcalm's southern impetuosity must be suspected. Bougainville was an hour and a half's march behind the enemy with 3,000 more men. In time Montcalm should have

been able to persuade the Governor to release men from Beauport and the city. It is said he feared that the British would be reinforced – there was nobody to reinforce them with, but he evidently did not realize that. At all events, the Marquis de Montcalm ordered a general advance at about 10 a.m. His line – regulars in the centre, mixed regulars, colony troops and militia on the flanks – came on steadily. The two British cannon which had been dragged up the cliffs, and the three French pieces from Quebec, plied the closing battle lines with grape and canister. The redcoats, who had been lying down to avoid this and the snipers' fire, now stood up and ordered their ranks. The white ranks approaching them became slightly ragged – the colony troops and militia were not used to this sort of manoeuvre and could not maintain their dressing; and the Canadians, following the habits of the forest, threw themselves down on the ground to reload after each shot, completely destroying the continuity of the lines. The British did not fire; they advanced a few paces, and waited. When the two armies were a mere forty yards apart, the order was given, and 'the most perfect volley ever fired' crashed out.

The traditional strength of the British infantry, the delayed, perfectly timed mass volley at short range, sounded like a single cannon shot. As the great bank of dirty grey-white smoke rolled forward and completely hid the armies from one another, a second volley followed, then a sharp period of 'fire at will'. The smoke lifted, and revealed a scene of carnage. The regulars of Old France lay writhing or still on the grass in their hundreds, and the disordered front wavered in confusion. The order to charge passed down the British line; some dashed forward firing, some with the bayonet, the Highlanders with the broadsword. The French retreated, some in panic, others more steadily and still firing. Wolfe was on the far right, with the unit of grenadiers detached from the regiments at Louisbourg. Urging on the advance, he was hit in the wrist. He wrapped a kerchief round the shattered joint and kept on. A second shot, in the body, staggered him; a third dropped him. He died a few minutes later in the arms of Grenadier Henderson, knowing that his army was victorious.

As the French retreat became more frenzied and

The wholly inaccurate painting of Montcalm's death by Vatteau; two of the more obvious absurdities are the placing of the General's death on the battlefield, and the palm-tree. (P. H. Gidaly)

less orderly, Montcalm was borne back in the crush towards the St Louis Gate. A shot passed through his body; the Royal Artillery later claimed it was grape from Captain York's cannon, but on what grounds it is hard to say. Held in his saddle by a soldier on either side, he rode his black horse through the St Louis Gate, blood streaming down. Some women of the city, clustering round, saw his wound and cried out, 'Mon Dieu, le Marquis est tué!' 'Ce n'est rien, ce n'est rien; ne vous affligez pas pour moi, mes bonnes amies,' he replied.

They took him to the house of Surgeon Arnoux; told that he had some twelve hours to live, he replied that he was happy he would not live to see the surrender of Quebec – which the poltroon Vaudreuil was abandoning to its fate. He gave certain advice on the military situation, and highly recommended his friend de Lévis as his successor. One of his last acts was to write to Brigadier Townshend, now the British commander

with Wolfe dead and Monckton disabled, interceding for the Canadian civilians. When the confused officers of the staff begged for his orders, he replied: 'I will neither give orders nor interfere any further. I have much business that must be attended to, of greater moment than your ruined garrison and this wretched country. My time is very short; therefore, pray leave me. I wish you all comfort, and to be happily extricated from your present perplexities.' He received the last sacraments from Bishop Pontbriand, and died at about four o'clock on the morning of 14 September 1759. Vaudreuil later wrote a letter to his Minister blaming all the misfortunes of the colony on the dead soldier, in terms which leave the reader sickened at the depths of meanness to which the human spirit can sink.

Just under one year later, on 8 September 1760, Vaudreuil signed the articles of capitulation by which Canada and all its dependencies passed to the British Crown.

The Plates

A Major-General the Marquis of Montcalm

Montcalm is shown here as he is believed to have appeared when rallying the French forces on the Plains of Abraham before the battle in which he was mortally wounded, on the morning of 13 September 1759. Eyewitnesses reported that he rode up and down ordering the French line of battle, on a black horse, with drawn sword. The cuirass, with lines of simple chiselled decoration as illustrated here, is an unusual feature at this late date; it is preserved at his family home, the Château de Candiac. French general officers of the day wore a prescribed uniform only when actually on campaign. It consisted of a single-breasted blue coat, a red waistcoat, and red or white breeches, with a black cocked hat decorated with gold lace trim and white plumage. The coat and waistcoat were richly embroidered with a 'folded' pattern of gold bullion lace. Decorations and orders were not generally worn with the campaign uniform. Heavy black leather riding-boots are worn; the sword-belt is of white leather with gold decoration, and the sword and scabbard are furnished in gilt metal and bullion cord.

B1 Canadian militiaman, Trois Rivières brigade, 1759

For the campaign of 1759 the militia companies were amalgamated into three brigades by region of origin, and wore the knitted *tuque* or stocking cap typical of the French *habitant* in different colours according to their brigade: red for Quebec, white for Trois Rivières, and blue for Montreal.

A much more authentic view – 'La Mort de Montcalm' by Suzor-Coté. The Marquis died in the early hours of the day after the battle, in the house of an absent Quebec surgeon. He was buried on the night of 14 September 1759, in a shell-hole in the floor of the wrecked chapel of the Ursuline convent in the city, which had suffered heavy damage from the British artillery. (Musée du Quebec/ N. Bazin).

This man's dress is otherwise completely non-military. The brown civilian coat, with low pockets and 'mariner's cuffs', is of rather archaic cut, as are the shoes with laced flaps. The woollen sash under the waist-belt was common wear in New France. The belt supports a bullet-bag and a 'butcher knife'. The powder flask slung from a cross-belt is thirty years out of date – a canny administration saved such old equipment for issue to the militia. The few personal effects are bundled into a simple bag and slung with rope. The musket is the excellent iron-mounted model of 1728, and the promise of keeping it, at an artificially low price, on his release from service was a major inducement to the unpaid militiaman.

B2 Fusilier, Compagnies Franches de la Marine, c. 1750
In about 1700 the men of the *Compagnies Franches* had worn the greyish-white French infantry coat – the *justaucorps* – with blue cuffs, and their hat lace and buttons had been false silver and pewter. The distinctions became false gold and brass about that period, and by 1740 the cuffs had changed to coat-colour. The cuffs of sergeants had a strip of gold lace round the top. The low stand-up collar is characteristic of this corps. The *justaucorps* is worn over a long-sleeved thigh-length waistcoat in royal blue; blue knee-breeches; and blue woollen stockings. The shirt is of white linen, collarless, with full sleeves gathered at the wrist. The stock and shoes are black leather. All buckles are brass. The stitched heart decorations on the coat-tails, which are hooked up for ease on the march, are typical of eighteenth-century military fashion, and were worn in several forms by men of several nations.

Equipment is slung on buff leather belts; the waist-belt has a double frog holding the scabbards of the sword and socket bayonet, and the cartridge-box is slung on the cross-belt. The sword is a straight, brass-hilted épée; both scabbards are covered with brown leather and tipped with brass. The leather *cartouchier* holds twenty-seven paper cartridges for the ·69-calibre smooth-bore musket, model 1728. The musket is 5 ft. 2½ in. long.

The illustration shows a local enlistee to the *Compagnies Franches*; his face is disfigured by one of the crude flower or animal tattoos common among the rougher element in New France. They were imprinted by burning gunpowder in the needle-wounds.

B3 Fusilier, Swiss Regiment 'Karrer', Louisbourg, 1745
The French have always made great use of mercenary regiments, and the Swiss have a long tradition of mercenary soldiering. The Karrer Regiment was raised for service in the colonies by the French Ministry of Marine in 1721; its companies served in Louisiana and the Caribbean as well as in Canada. In 1745 two companies served as part of the garrison of Louisbourg, and were apparently on the verge of mutiny due to the bad living conditions. The fortress fell to Pepperell's provincials in 1745; the garrison fought bravely, but had little chance. There were no

The *pakalem* or fatigue cap of the French troops. The cap was always the same colour as the regimental waistcoat, with frontal badge, braiding and tassel in white or yellow according to the colour of the regimental buttons and hat lace. (G. A. Embleton)

proper stocks of necessary supplies, and many of the emplacements had no cannon.

This fusilier – that is, a private soldier of a company other than the grenadier company – is illustrated as he would appear on sentry duty on the windswept ramparts, at the drill position known as 'Portez l'arme au bras'. He has added locally-made scarf and mittens to his uniform in the dreary Nova Scotian winter. His black cocked hat has a black ribbon cockade in the usual infantry fashion, and white tape 'lace'. The red justaucorps is characteristic of Swiss units in French service; its blue collar, cuffs, and lining and white metal buttons, and the peculiar cut of the pockets, are all regimental distinctions. It is worn over a royal blue waistcoat and breeches, and this sentry wears the standard-issue white canvas gaiters, fastened with buttons and a knee-strap, worn by all French infantry in the field and for drill. His 1717 Charleville musket, buff leather equipment, sword, bayonet, and pouch are all standard-issue items.

C1 Fusilier, Compagnies Franches, winter campaign dress, 1750s

The physical conditions made winter campaigning by large units of regular troops impossible in America, and the regulars were usually pulled back to the heart of Canada and put into winter quarters. A war of patrol and ambush, escort and scouting took the place of large scale operations; and in these expeditions the men of the colony troops joined the coureurs de bois and the Indians.

The hair and beard were probably worn long, for comfort. The traditional tuque is worn, as is the capote or heavy unbleached blanket-coat. With a hood, and decorative fringes and bands of simple colours, this was normal wear for soldiers and civilians alike. Moccasins and fancy leggings or mitasses, here of wool but often of blanket or hide, were normal patrol wear. Indian garters were often worn, such as the Ojibway ones illustrated here; and the ceinture flèche, or fancy coloured sash, was also popular.

Bulky and unnecessary equipment has been abandoned; the cartridge-box is worn centrally on a waist-belt, and a hatchet replaces sword and bayonet for hand-to-hand fighting. (The hand-axe was the normal close combat weapon among French, English, American, and Indian alike.) Rations and spare clothing are carried in the de la Parterie pack, a simple linen bag with the flap tied down over a strap. Snow-shoes – raquettes – were standard issue to the colony troops; and this soldier carries ice-creepers, the simple iron crampons which were tied to the shoes to ease movement over the frozen lakes and rivers.

C2 Fusilier, Compagnies Franches, summer fatigue dress, 1750s

A colony soldier as he might appear in peace time or far from the fighting, eking out his meagre pay from a corrupt administration by working the land of a local seigneur. His tools are copied from items excavated in Canada. The hollow, plugged gourd was a popular form of home-made water-canteen in the eighteenth century. The pipe was as ubiquitous as the modern soldier's fag-end – it is recorded that practically every male in New France chain-smoked from the age of twelve up. The black stock was hardly ever removed, and one may assume that this soldier's sergeant is far away. He wears the normal warm-weather working and fighting dress – the coat has been laid aside, and he wears only the long-sleeved veste and breeches, with his canvas gaiters partially unbuttoned for ease of movement. If he appears to be physically substandard, it should be born in mind that the only medical requirements of the Compagnies Franches were a height of 4 ft. 10 in., and enough teeth to be able to survive on winter rations, which were not of gourmet quality.

C3 Coureur de bois, 1750s

A 'woods-runner' of the type who proved such invaluable scouts for Montcalm's army, and such ruthless raiders of outlying British settlements. In mixed war-parties with Indians, a few colony troops, militia, and perhaps a few adventurous young chevaliers, they left a trail of red havoc along the frontier, and their standards of behaviour towards prisoners were little higher than those of the Indians. The better guerilla leaders, such as Marin and Charles Langlade, were of great help to Montcalm, but even they could not control the tribesmen with any certainty.

This fierce trapper is clad in a shapeless fur cap, and fringed buckskin hunting-shirt and leggings worn with a breech-cloth in the Indian fashion. A deerskin pouch decorated with coloured quills contains his few necessities – dried meat trail rations, bullets and flints, spare moccasins, etc. A tomahawk, a carved and stained powder-horn, and a rather elderly dog-lock musket, complete his worldly possessions. The hair and beard are untrimmed; braids and earrings were popular.

D1 Fusilier, Régiment de Béarn, 1755–60
Formed originally from elements of the Picardie Regiment in 1684, the Béarn saw much action under Montcalm; it was present at all major engagements of the campaign. It was disbanded after repatriation in 1760.

This fusilier is in the drill position, 'Remettez la bagrette en son lieu' – just returning the iron ramrod to its pipes after loading the musket. His hair is carefully queued and powdered, and the coat-skirts are not hooked up as was usual on campaign – he appears as he might when in Montreal or Quebec for the winter. The usual grey-white *justaucorps* and breeches of the French regular infantry are enlivened by certain regimental distinctions. A red *veste* is worn, and the coat has a red turn-down collar and red cuffs with three buttons; all buttons, and the hat lace, are of yellow metal finish. The shape of the pockets is another regimental distinction. Arms and equipment are standard issue.

D2 Grenadier, Régiment de La Reine, with battalion colour: 1755–60
Though no longer used for their original function, grenadier companies still figured on the establishment of French infantry battalions, and were still the 'shock troops', hand-picked from the biggest and strongest recruits. At Ticonderoga Montcalm detached all the grenadiers and held them as a reserve behind the main defensive line. Grenadier companies still enjoyed minor uniform distinctions. The men were encouraged to wear moustaches, while other soldiers had to be clean-shaven. Two items of equipment peculiar to

grenadiers were issued: a broad-tipped curved sabre in place of the straight épée sword, and a larger and more ornate pouch. Although referred to as a grenade-pouch, this was used for carrying cartridges in the usual way.

This grenadier's grey-white coat and breeches are distinguished by a red collar and cuffs, white metal buttons, false silver hat trim, and distinctive eight-button pocket flaps peculiar to this regiment alone. The *veste* is blue. On campaign the hair was pulled back into the usual black bow, then wrapped into a tight pigtail bound with leather, cloth, or eel-skin. The equipment is unremarkable apart from the grenadier items. The colour, of which each battalion had one when on detached service, is that of the regiment. The pike has a brass head and is decorated with a white silk scarf and gold tasselled cords; these were often removed and stowed away when in the field – unlike the colour, they were paid for out of the colonel's pocket.

D3 Officer, Corps of Engineers, 1750s
Despite the popular image of the American fort, all pointed tree-trunks and rustic woodwork, the major forts of the French/Indian Wars were constructed on conventional European lines using local materials; and professional engineers, with a proper grasp of the science brought to such a high peak of expertise by Vauban, were necessary members of any general's staff. The reconnaissance and evaluation of the enemy's positions fell within the engineer's task, as much as the surveying of sites and laying out of one's own batteries and bastions; for two centuries the engineer officer was to have a function with much of the intelligence officer about it. Montcalm lost a valued engineer in Descombles, tomahawked by a 'friendly' Indian while reconnoitring Fort Ontario for his chief; the Indian placed as much value on his scalp as Montcalm did upon his brain.

The engineer illustrated here wears the royal colours of his corps, the blue coat lined and collared in red. A particular distinction of the engineers was the black plush velvet cuff; and the gilt buttons are arranged in fives. The *veste* and breeches are red, and the sword-belt is the usual officer's pattern.

E1 Sergeant, Régiment de Royal-Roussillon, 1756–60
Dressed for duty in town or camp, this N.C.O. wears his waist-belt and sword slung over his shoulder – a popular fashion among soldiers of the day. He carries his halberd of rank, but this would certainly have been replaced by a musket on campaign. (Grenadier sergeants carried muskets in place of halberds at all times.) The *justaucorps*, worn with a blue *veste*, has blue collar and cuffs; the pocket shape, the six-button cuffs, the yellow metal buttons, and the false gold hat trim are all regimental distinctions. The lace around the top of the cuff is the sergeant's insignia of rank.

E2 Corporal, Régiment de Guyenne, marching order, 1755–60
The *justaucorps* of this regiment had red collar and cuffs; the waistcoat was red, the buttons brass, and the hat was trimmed with false gold. The pockets had a simple three-button flap. The insignia of corporal's rank in the Guyenne were three strips of yellow worsted lace arranged vertically on the three-button cuff.

This N.C.O. is dressed for a long day's march in the wilderness. His hair is not powdered, and is plaited for convenience. His sword has been left 'in store', and instead he has a hatchet slipped into the straps of his *cartouchier*. Heart-shaped designs decorate the hooked-up coat-skirts. The *de la Parterie* pack contains rations and spare clothing: staple fare included biscuit, salt pork or salt cod, and split peas, but officers received brandy and chocolate in addition. An extra pair of moccasins and a small camp-kettle are slung on the outside. The bundle of poles tied with rope are the frame for the four-man squad tent.

E3 Mission Indian, 1750s
The 'Christian' Hurons of Lorette, the Abenakis from St Francis, and the Iroquois of La Présentation, were the most consistent of France's unruly native allies, and their Jesuit priests exerted much control, by various means; a not unusual means is attracting this warrior's interest. A minor chief or *sachem*, he has been given a French officer's gorget to wear round his neck as a mark of authority. Old laced European coats were apparently much prized among the Indians; this one has unbuttoned the deep cuffs of his too-short sleeves. The coat is worn with the traditional hide leggings and moccasins, and a breech-cloth. The necklaces of beads and claws, and the stretched earlobes with brass ornaments, are mentioned by contemporary writers. The battered British Army tin canteen is, perhaps, a souvenir of the fall of Fort William Henry, when the mission Indians led the massacre of prisoners.

F1 Corporal, Régiment de La Sarre, off-duty dress, 1756–60
A not untypical sight around Ticonderoga, Frontenac, and Niagara in the late 1750s; an officer of the Languedoc wrote of '... nothing but pease and bacon on the mess-table. Luckily the lakes are full of fish, and both officers and soldiers have to turn fishermen.' For an afternoon's angling this N.C.O., his rank indicated by the

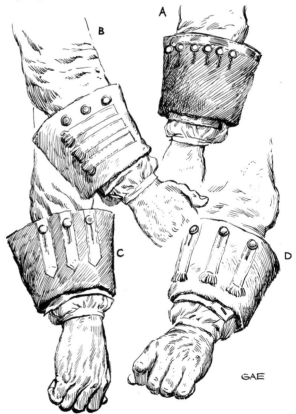

Cuff lace of French regular N.C.O.s: (A) the gold lace stripe of a sergeant in the Régiment de Royal-Roussillon; (B) the yellow worsted stripes of a corporal in the Béarn; (C) the yellow worsted loops of a corporal in the La Sarre; and (D) the yellow loops of a corporal of the Guyenne. (G. A. Embleton, courtesy *Tradition*)

loops of worsted lace on his cuffs, wears the *pakalem* fatigue cap. Regimental distinctions include a red *veste* and a *justaucorps* with blue collar and cuffs, and brass buttons.

F2 Company Officer, *Régiment de Berry, Quebec, 1757*
A young *chevalier* newly arrived from France, in drill uniform. Apart from the superior quality and cut of the material his grey-white coat and breeches are the same as those worn by his men. His red regimental *veste* with a double row of gilt buttons is embroidered with gold lace to indicate commissioned rank. Regimental distinctions include gilt buttons and gilt hat-lace, the unusual double

French infantry equipment of the 1750s. The small, plain cartridge-boxes are fusilier styles, the large one with the royal arms stamped on the flap is the grenadier pouch. The double frog holds a fusilier's épée and bayonet, and a grenadier's sabre is shown on the right. All leather belts were buff-coloured and all metal furniture brass. (G. A. Embleton)

vertical coat pockets, a red collar and red cuffs with five buttons. The black stock of the common soldier was sometimes worn in the field, but in garrison the officer wore a white neckcloth, with fine lace at the throat of the shirt. The white gaiters were worn for drill. The gorget is a sign of commissioned rank, as is the espontoon or half-pike – it was used, like the sergeant's halberd, to dress the ranks and to signal evolutions. The sword, with gilt furniture, is slung from a white stitched leather belt.

F3 Fusilier, *Régiment de La Reine, summer campaign dress, 1758*
The equipment is worn directly over the blue regimental *veste* with white metal buttons, which made a comfortable and neat summer uniform. He has discarded his sword, and carries his musket casually reversed. The only notable thing about his dress is his replacement of the hat cockade with a bunch of feathers. The cockades were often lost or spoiled by weather, and the soldier was expected to purchase another; feathers, hanks of coloured thread, or even leaves were popular and cheaper alternatives. The La Reine fought under de Lévis at the north end of the Ticonderoga breastwork, where the 42nd Highlanders made their famous charge. After the battle, this fusilier examines a Black Watch grenadier cap he has picked up off the field.

G1 Drummer, *Régiment de Guyenne, 1755–60*
This company drummer wears the uniform common to musicians of all the regular regiments in Canada except the La Reine. Drummers wore the 'King's livery' – a blue coat with red distinctions. Coat and *veste* were generously trimmed, down the front edges, on the buttonholes, and along all main seams, with a special pattern of lace: red, with a white 'chain' motif. The 'King's' regiments were also distinguished by the blue bodies of the drums themselves. The drummers of La Reine wore the 'Queen's livery' – red coats trimmed with blue, blue lace with a white 'chain', and red drums with blue and white diagonally striped counter-

hoops. The drum is decorated with trophies of arms and representations of the regimental colours supporting the royal arms. When in use it is carried hooked to a broad leather sling with metal terminals, and on the march it is slung on the back by the plaited cord. This drummer has substituted a bunch of autumn leaves for a mislaid cockade. He is armed with a sword only.

G2 Company officer, *Régiment de Languedoc, summer campaign dress, 1758*

When campaigning in the forests the French line officers soon discovered the wisdom of adopting a practical but neat form of dress, similar to what they would wear for a day's shooting on their French estates. This officer has laid aside his coat and fights in his richly embroidered regimental *veste*, with gilt buttons. The plush velvet breeches – a harder-wearing material than that known as velvet today – were very popular among officers of the day, being both sturdy and comfortable. The legs are well protected by infantry officer's campaign gaiters, robust leggings made of stiff black leather, and fastened with brass buckles up the outside. This officer retains his white leather sword-belt and regulation sword; and the gorget of rank would never be discarded. His hat is trimmed with the gold lace of his regiment. His weapon is a fine flintlock fusil, probably his personal hunting weapon, although such guns were issued to officers by the army. It is much shorter and lighter than a musket. He carries ammunition in a fusilier's cartridge-box of normal pattern, and fine-grain powder for his superior flintlock in a silver-mounted horn.

G3 Woods Indian Warrior, *1750s*

'I see no difference,' Bougainville wrote, 'in the dress, ornaments, dances, and songs of the various western nations. They go naked, excepting a strip of cloth passed through a belt. . . .' A missionary writes: 'Imagine a great assembly of savages adorned with every ornament most suited to disfigure them in European eyes, painted with vermilion, white, green, yellow, and black . . . methodically laid on with the help of a little tallow,

which serves for pomatum. The head is shaved except at the top, where there is a small tuft, to which are fastened feathers, a few beads of wampum, or some such trinket. . . . Pendants hang from the nose and also from the ears, which are split in infancy and drawn down with weights till they flap at last against the shoulders . . . !' Knives were worn hanging from the neck, and pierced silver discs were popular gifts and trade currency. Here, the buckskin leggings worn in close country are allowed to hang down over the knee-garters. Many of the wild Indians were armed with flint arrows and spears, and by no means all had guns. This warrior has just acquired a rather elderly flintlock of late seventeenth-century pattern, in a raid on some frontier settlement. The 'curved swastika' pattern on the armlet was a popular decorative motif. The knife is a European trade item.

H1 Cadet-Gentilhomme, *Corps Royal d'Artillerie, 1757*

An artillery company had served at Louisbourg since 1743, and this was supplemented in 1750 by raising a second from promising men of the *Compagnies Franches*. In 1757 twenty officers and men were sent from France to reinforce the small artillery contingent. The unskilled work of handling the guns was probably carried out by infantry and militia. The royal colours are worn: a blue coat with red distinctions, with five brass buttons on the pockets and four on the cuffs; *veste* and breeches were also red, with a double row of buttons for enlisted men and a single row for officers. This gentleman-cadet, learning the martial arts in the field, wears the basic uniform of a common soldier distinguished by a knot of yellow worsted cords at the right shoulder. He has a large master-gunner's powder-horn, of the type used to prime cannon, and holds a combination powder-scoop and worm. *Cadets-gentilhommes* were under the orders of N.C.O.s but were excused fatigues.

H2 Grenadier, *Régiment de Cambis, Louisbourg, 1755*

Off duty and dicing away his pay, this soldier wears his hat pushed well forward in the currently fashionable manner. His red regimental *veste* hangs in the characteristic way when unfastened. The black stock is worn. The shirt is linen, collarless, full and pleated; it is a pullover style, split half-way down the chest. The white knee-breeches have a typical flap front; the soldier wears a belt for convenience, though it was not regulation. In the barracks he does not wear his canvas gaiters over the woollen stockings and buckled shoes. The ubiquitous clay pipe was often broken off short for convenience in the field, and carried in a leather pouch round the neck. The *justaucorps* of the Cambis had a red collar and cuffs, the latter with three buttons, two of white metal and the centre one in brass. This style was repeated on the pocket flap.

H3 Grenadier, Régiment de Languedoc, 1755–60
This grenadier, with the moustache of his privileged status, is in full uniform and issue equipment, including the grenadier sabre. He is in the drill position, 'Déchirez la cartouche avec les dents' – tearing the paper cartridge open with his teeth, in order to pour powder into the pan and then insert the rest of the cartridge into the muzzle of the musket. He wears a *justaucorps* with regimental distinctions; blue collar and cuffs, brass buttons (four on the cuffs), and six-button pockets. The *veste* is blue, the hat lace false gold. Yet another variation on the heart motif is stitched to the coat-tails; little brass hearts were sometimes attached to the cloth.